MAKE
AHEAD
MEALS

MICHAEL SMITH

MAKE AHEAD MEALS

OVER 100 EASY TIME-SAVING RECIPES

Photography by Ryan Szulc

PENGUIN

an imprint of Penguin Canada Books Inc., a Penguin Random House Company

Published by the Penguin Group

Penguin Canada Books Inc., 320 Front Street West,
   Toronto, Ontario M5V 3B6, Canada

Penguin Group (USA) Inc., 375 Hudson Street, New York, New York 10014, U.S.A.

Penguin Books Ltd, 80 Strand, London WC2R 0RL, England

Penguin Ireland, 25 St Stephen's Green, Dublin 2, Ireland (a division of Penguin Books Ltd)

Penguin Group (Australia), 707 Collins Street, Melbourne, Victoria 3008, Australia
   (a division of Pearson Australia Group Pty Ltd)

Penguin Books India Pvt Ltd, 11 Community Centre, Panchsheel Park,
   New Delhi – 110 017, India

Penguin Group (NZ), 67 Apollo Drive, Rosedale, Auckland 0632, New Zealand
   (a division of Pearson New Zealand Ltd)

Penguin Books (South Africa) (Pty) Ltd, 24 Sturdee Avenue, Rosebank,
   Johannesburg 2196, South Africa

Penguin Books Ltd, Registered Offices: 80 Strand, London WC2R 0RL, England

First published 2015

1 2 3 4 5 6 7 8 9 10   (C&C)

Food photography by Ryan Szulc
Food styling by Noah Witenoff
Prop styling by Madeleine Johari

Manufactured in China.

LIBRARY AND ARCHIVES CANADA CATALOGUING IN PUBLICATION

Smith, Michael, author
     Make ahead meals / Michael Smith.

Includes index.
ISBN 978-0-14-319216-9 (pbk.)

     1. Make-ahead cooking. 2. Cooking. 3. Cookbooks.
I. Title.

TX714.S599 2015   641.5'55   C2015-900953-7

eBook ISBN 978-0-14-319614-3

Visit the Penguin Canada website at www.penguin.ca

Special and corporate bulk purchase rates available; please see www.penguin.ca/corporatesales
or call 1-800-810-3104.

This cookbook is dedicated to every flavor-loving cook looking for solid time-saving cook-ahead strategies today and to their families and friends who get to enjoy the results tomorrow!

ALSO BY
MICHAEL SMITH

CONTENTS

INTRODUCTION

Spend time gathering and preparing food now to save time sharing it later. Life is busy. Sometimes we—and our kitchens—have a hard time keeping up. We all intend to cook from scratch and eat healthily, but our schedules can really limit our options.

Cooking ahead is an easy and affordable way to push back schedule pressure and keep your family's diet on track. Plan ahead. Prep dishes ahead so you can finish them easily when the time comes. Or cook full meals in advance and chill them or freeze them. Life may be busy, but you can still impress yourself in your own kitchen!

Every chef knows how to super-charge their kitchen by getting organized. I helped build my career that way and bring that energy home. You can too by doing just a few basic things. A smart shopping-list system speeds up your shopping cart and guarantees you won't forget anything. A well laid out kitchen with a space for everything boosts productivity. This is especially important in the pantry, refrigerator and freezer. You might have to invest some time to reorganize your kitchen, but you'll be glad you did.

Make Ahead Meals includes many recipes, ideas and tips for strategically getting ahead of your cooking. There are many ways not just to save time but to bring wholesomeness to your table. Part of our job as cooks is to keep our families away from the nutritional emptiness of processed food. Cook ahead and process your own! Save time—and eat well!

As a very busy dad who still routinely cooks for my beautiful wife and family, I fully understand the challenges we all face as home cooks. I'm thrilled to share with you hard-earned lessons from the front lines of my home kitchen and crazy schedule. You don't have to let your busy schedule get in the way of a healthy diet. Take a deep breath, get organized and cook ahead!

Spend Time to Save Time

1. **GET ORGANIZED** Be deliberate. Start small and ramp up. Begin by absorbing this list of the benefits and strategies of cooking ahead. A small amount of effort organizing yourself now will produce large and growing results downstream.

2. **SUPERCHARGE YOUR KITCHEN** Organize everything, from pots and pans to bowls, tools and utensils. Sharpen your knives and store them safely. Organize your pantry shelves, your fridge and your freezer. Plan ahead, be consistent and always maintain a shopping list—and use it. And remember to enjoy yourself and take pride in being an organized pro!

3. **MEAL PLANNING** Think ahead. Set up a weekly meal plan that works for you and your family. Jot down the week's menu on the back of your shopping list for easy reference when you're shopping. Before you head to the store, double-check that you've listed all the ingredients you need.

4. **NEW FLAVORS** Try new dishes. Be fresh. It's fun and will keep you motivated! Keep making your family's favorite dishes, of course, but be sure to regularly introduce new ones. Try not to get stuck in a rut. There are so many dishes out there just waiting to be discovered and become new family favorites.

   You might enjoy recipes like Vietnamese Chicken Curry (page 104), Korean Short Ribs (page 119) and Baked Reuben Chowder (page 60).

5. **PREPARE AND FINISH** Many dishes can easily be prepared days in advance, then quickly finished with a last-minute flourish of fresh flavor. With practice you'll be able to two-step just about any recipe.

   You might enjoy recipes like Yesterday's Tomato Saffron Broth, Today's Fish (page 132), Amazing Morning Microwave Muffins (page 14) and Homemade Soda Pop (page 220).

6. **AFTER-SUPPER PREPARATION** Many cooks are understandably focused on the critical window between their arrival home and their first bite—the faster the better. So always think ahead. Every day, as soon as dinner is over, prepare whatever you can for tomorrow. This strategy will perpetually speed up dinner.

   You might enjoy recipes like Fall Flavors Salad (page 47), Coffee Spice Crusted Steak with Chipotle Chimichurri (page 114) and Slow-Roasted Cherry Tomatoes, Grapes and Pearl Onions (page 147).

7. **WEEKEND MAKE AHEAD RALLY** Fire up your kitchen for a few hours and simultaneously cook supper plus one or two other meals for the freezer. Get organized and enjoy yourself. You'll be surprised how much you can pull off once you're up and running.

You might enjoy recipes like Honey-Spiced Roast Turkey Leftovers (page 98), Bacon Cheddar Stuffed Potatoes (page 153) and Everyday Whole-Grain Bread (page 20).

8. **DOUBLE BATCH** It's usually just as easy to double a dish—saving one meal for next time—as it is to make just one for now. Many dishes can be doubled or even tripled, and you'll quickly discover how much efficiency you gain this way.

You might enjoy recipes like Prosciutto Lemon Wrapped Chicken (page 111), Mulligatawny Quinoa (page 158) and San Marzano Marinara Sauce (page 169).

9. **SAVE SMALL MEALS** You can divide many dishes into multiple smaller frozen portions poised for a hot lunchbox meal or even another dinner. If you prepare two or three dishes simultaneously, you can rally lunch for a month.

You might enjoy recipes like Sweet Potato Soup and Pumpkin Seed Pesto (page 67), El Paso Shepherd's Pie (page 117) and Black Olive Baba Ghanoush and Mini Pita Chips (page 37).

10. **COOKING CLUB** Pick your favorite dish and a fun theme. Fill your freezer with a portion for everyone. Gather your foodie friends and organize a monthly swap meet. Encourage them to interpret the theme and share their frozen favorites.

You might enjoy recipes like Vegetarian Minestrone (page 58), Tex-Mex Chipotle Chicken Filling (page 193) and Dulce de Leche Coconut Squares (page 228).

SHOPPING LIST

- Bananas
- Plain Yogurt
- Orange Juice
- Coconut Milk
- Sandwich Stuff
- Whole Wheat
- Baking Powder
- Molasses
- Chick Peas
- San Marzano
-

Your Shopping List

1. **USE YOUR COMPUTER** Create a template checklist of your own or download mine from chefmichaelsmith.com. (Look under *Make Ahead Meals* on the "Cookbooks" page.) It's easy to use, and you can change it to suit your needs. Within each category, include lots of example prompts and lots of blanks for new ideas too. If you buy a particular product consistently, include its name. Update the document frequently as your habits and tastes evolve. You'll find that it really helps you stay organized.

2. **SMART CATEGORIES** Organize your list with specific categories that follow your path through your favorite grocery store. Include fresh produce, meat, fish, dairy, dry goods, frozen and any other sections that fit your world. Oh, and leave the processed-food aisles off your list.

3. **PRINT AND POST** Print your shopping list, post it somewhere useful and use it every day. Try to write down everything you run out of or you're running low on. Before you head to the market, glance through the categories, read any recipes ahead, and double-check your shelves.

4. **MEAL PLANNING** I like to jot down the week's menu on the back of my shopping list and read through any new recipes before I go shopping. My family's meal plan includes meat, fish and lots of vegetables, so a list really helps us keep on track. And a menu can help you add new ideas or ingredients. Try designating one night a week for fish, vegetarian, pasta, global, a special request or something brand new.

5. **INCLUDE AMOUNTS** Don't forget to give yourself lots of specific notes on amounts and types of items when you need to. A lot of things you buy every time you go grocery shopping, and you know how much you'll need. But if you're trying a new dish and an ingredient is unfamiliar, jot down the exact amount you need. You don't want to get home and discover you have too little!

6. **FLEXIBLE FLAVORS** Leave room for improvisation. Allow yourself to be inspired by fresh, in-season fruits and vegetables. Look for new ones and choose the freshest, modifying your menu plan as needed. Don't feel locked in to the demands of a recipe: if it calls for something tired and something fresher catches your eye, be bold!

7. **SMART CART** When you know you're going for a really big shop, start with heavier packaged goods in your cart and reserve the top section for delicate items. Finish with lighter fresh produce on top of the works.

8. **STORE DEALS** Keep an eye on the flyers and look for display signs as you roam the store. You may spot a special deal or two. If so, buy two or three and freeze a few.

9. **BUY IN BULK** I visit our local Bulk Barn at least once a month. I save money buying in bulk, but more importantly I'm inspired by the vast selection of flavors. We eat lots of nuts, grains and legumes, so it makes sense to buy them in bulk.

10. **HIGHLIGHTER CHECK-OFF** To me shopping is like big game hunting. I search the aisles high and low for elusive prey and secretly take great pleasure in striking each item from the list with my trusty yellow highlighter. The finished list is a trophy of sorts for me! If you take the time to check off what's in your cart, you'll be sure to not forget anything.

Pantry Shelves

1. **GLOBAL FLAVOR GALLERY** Surround yourself with the flavors of the world, poised to prepare any exotic dish from afar. As you try new dishes, you'll begin accumulating ingredients in various forms. Sort them into categories. Keep them organized. When you're looking for dinner inspiration, you'll know where to find it!

2. **MASON JARS** For inspiration, I like to see my ingredients. I sort the many raw ingredients and prepared flavors that flow through my kitchen into various-sized clear mason jars. We have lots and have many uses for them—even as our standard water glasses.

3. **HERBS AND DRIED SPICES** I really enjoy maintaining a simple library of mason jars filled with the many and various herbs and spices that fill my cooking with flavor. I like knowing I have at least a little bit of just about everything, from allspice to za'atar. Leaves, seeds, flowers, bark, pods and powders—I've got them in my pantry and you can too. Have fun getting set up, then find inspiration from them and get cooking.

4. **POTATOES, ROOTS, ONIONS AND GARLIC** Root-cellar ingredients appreciate a quiet, cool, dark place. Store them well and they'll stay fresh. A closed pantry with the light off or a plain bin with a tight-fitting lid will help. Keep your garlic in a basket with a roller peeler ready to go. When you need some peeled garlic, work the cloves over the basket to contain the inevitable mess.

5. **RIPENING FRUIT** So many fruits benefit from careful ripening. You can really increase their flavor and nutritional intensity with deliberate ripening of bananas, melons, mangoes, peaches, pears, plums, apricots, pineapples and other tropical fruits. They all deserve to become their best, and with a little patience you'll be rewarded with peak flavor and nutrients. It's as simple as resting them neatly on platters or in bowls and checking them daily for freshness. You'll know when they're ripe.

6. **DRIED GRAINS, LEGUMES AND STAPLES** These raw ingredients are the most affordable and reliable in your kitchen, and stocking a basic pantry is easy. Grains, wheats, rices, flours, popcorn, dried beans, dried lentils, dried pastas—keep them on hand and you'll always be ready to build dinner on the fly.

7. **CANNED CHICKPEAS AND BEANS** Stockpile goodness with a variety of canned whole chickpeas and any of the many canned bean types. They're all full of essential protein and easily incorporated into an array of dishes.

8. **CANNED TOMATOES** Except in late summer, when local tomatoes are bursting with flavor, canned tomatoes are an essential kitchen ingredient. A can of tomatoes anchors so many of the world's great dishes. Whether whole, diced, puréed or paste, you'll find their true field-ripe flavor far superior to that of the ubiquitous "fresh" so-called tomatoes. Select low-sodium versions and choose organic if you can.

9. **BAKE SHOP** One of life's great joys is the fine art and craft of patient, tasty baking. Its many techniques, tools and ingredients constitute a class unto themselves, and each deserves its own gathering and storing place. Various flours and sugars, baking powder and baking soda, yeast, butter (room-temperature and frozen), chocolate chips ... Organize yourself. You'll take pride in your setup and you'll be a better baker for it.

10. **ANCHOVIES** Of all the ingredients on my pantry shelves, the single most important is my ever-replenished stack of canned anchovies. Chazz loves my intense Caesar salad, and I toss an entire can into every batch of dressing, an investment that can get me out of just about any jam. You may not like them as much as we do, but whatever your favorite ingredient happens to be, make sure you have lots!

Fill the Fridge

1. **A CHILLY STRATEGY** Cooks have always valued refrigeration for its preservative properties. Cold has a slowing effect on the bacterial growth that can lead to spoilage. It's not infallible, though. Pay extra attention to your meat and fish, especially if you intend to prep a dish and cook it a day or two later. Use your eyes, nose and common sense, because you can't restart the freshness clock.

2. **ORGANIZE YOUR FRIDGE** Don't take your fridge and freezer for granted: maximize their effectiveness by organizing them and keeping them that way. Take a close look at all the various ingredients in your fridge and think about how they can easily be divided into categories. Then, dedicate various areas of the fridge to accommodate them—for example, fresh produce, store-bought and homemade condiments, beverages, meat, fish, and leftovers. Be specific and consistent and you'll quickly form a great habit that will help your efficiency in the long run.

3. **QUICK COOLING** When you're done heating a dish and don't intend to eat it immediately, cool it as quickly as possible. Time really is of the essence: the faster freshly prepared food plunges through the temperature danger zone to the safety of cold, the better the food will taste and the longer you can store it safely. Don't give bacteria a chance to grow. Immediately divide piping-hot food into shallow containers and get them in your fridge. Forget what your mother told you: modern fridges can handle hot food.

4. **TEMPERATURE RANGE** Buy a reliable refrigerator thermometer and keep an eye on your refrigerator's temperature. Food is best stored at just above its freezing point, at 35°F to 40°F (2°C to 4°C) or so. As its temperature rises, so does bacterial activity. At prolonged room temperature, bacteria are perilously active. It's only once heated past 145°F (65°C) that food returns to safety, but its quality can be severely damaged by improper handling.

5. **DON'T OVERFILL** Fridges work best when they're full but not stuffed. Most function by pulling air away from the contents, more efficiently cooling it and forming a slight vacuum in the process. Lots of ingredients filling that space means less air needs to move to maintain a constant temperature, so the fridge works more efficiently. But too many ingredients stuffed into nooks and crannies can impede airflow and efficiency.

6. **STORE MEAT AND FISH ON BOTTOM** It's wise to be hyper-conscious of the raw juices of the various meats and fish in your fridge. They have the potential to cross-contaminate other foods and make you very sick. Store meats and fish separately in their original store packaging, and store them in the bottom of your fridge so they don't drip on or in anything and spoil it.

7. **CONTAINERS AND TIGHT WRAPPING** Master the art of packaging. Reusable and resealable plastic containers are very useful, as is plastic wrap. Your aim is to limit constant airflow that can dry food and draw flavors and freshness from it.

8. **LEFTOVERS** Refrigerate any leftovers within an hour or so of cooking. Transfer them to containers and tightly seal them to preserve their flavor and moisture. Label them well or you may forget what's inside. Store them for just a few days, not more than five or six.

9. **HOW TO SAFELY THAW FOOD** Prepared food and raw meat and fish is best thawed over several days in the refrigerator, rather than on the counter at room temperature, where bacteria thrive. Plan ahead so you don't find yourself under pressure to thaw quickly and unsafely.

10. **WHAT IS SPOILAGE?** Food spoils through natural microbial processes that cause it to decay. It can fill with live bacteria that change textures and create unpalatable flavors, even harmful toxins. Bacterial activity slows down under refrigeration but speeds up dramatically at more comfortable room temperature. Refrigerate for both safety and flavor.

Freeze Ahead

1. **HOW DOES FREEZING WORK?** Fresh real food is alive and will naturally deteriorate over time. Refrigeration slows down the process, and freezing stops it completely. Once food is thawed, though, microorganisms will pick up right where they left off and begin growing again. To preserve quality, the secret is to freeze food at the peak of its freshness, before bacteria have had a chance to get going.

2. **FREEZE FAST** Freeze food quickly to preserve its flavor, because slow freezing can dry out food. As food freezes, tiny ice crystals form, and their jagged edges tear and puncture the surrounding cell walls. When the food thaws, it will literally leak moisture and lose flavor. The faster you can freeze the food, the smaller and less damaging those ice crystals will be. Your best bet is to flatten food as much as possible—even pour soups and stews into shallow containers—to help it freeze faster.

3. **INDIVIDUALLY FROZEN PIECES** Small food items frozen together will form a large, unmanageable lump. Instead, place things like meatballs, dumplings or portioned cookie dough separately on a lined baking sheet, freeze until solid, then transfer to a tightly sealed container for long-term storage.

4. **SMART PORTIONING** Freeze food in useful portions. Sometimes that means an entire pan containing a meal for many—a lasagna or casserole. Sometimes it makes sense to first divide the dish into smaller portions—say, for two or four—and freeze those. That way, you can conveniently pull out supper for one night—or one person.

5. **TIGHTLY SEAL FOOD TO PREVENT FREEZER BURN** Your freezer works by removing air from the compartment to more efficiently chill the works. This slight vacuum and constant air flow easily dry out any exposed food surfaces. Tightly wrapping and sealing prevents this deterioration. You'll notice a big difference between something stored in a bowl barely covered with a bit of loose plastic wrap and something in a tightly sealed heavy-duty freezer bag or plastic container.

6. **LABEL CLEARLY** Freezers have a funny way of filling up with unknown mystery leftovers that never seem to get used up and always take up too much space. Keep a roll of painter's tape and a marker handy and clearly label and date everything you freeze.

7. **HOW LONG CAN YOU FREEZE FOOD?** You can safely freeze most foods for years or more, but that's not the real issue. Quality is. Over time, food tends to dry out and lose flavor and vitality. Some foods are more durable than others, but eventually all foods reach their limit. Assuming they are very tightly sealed:

    - Vegetables: 1 year
    - Fruits: 1 year
    - Whole meat: 1 year
    - Portioned meat: 6 months
    - Fish: 6 months
    - Ground meat: 2 to 3 months
    - Breads and pastry: 2 to 3 months
    - Prepared foods: 2 to 3 months

8. **THAW SLOWLY** It's unsafe to thaw most foods—especially those containing meat and fish—at room temperature. Doing so exposes parts of the food to long periods of bacteria-friendly room temperature. It's better to plan ahead and thaw slowly in your refrigerator.

9. **DON'T REFREEZE MEAT OR FISH** Raw meat and fish can endure only one cycle of freezing and thawing. A second cycle will irrevocably damage texture and moisture content. It's not a question of safety so much as quality, so if you really have to, go ahead and refreeze—just know that on the other side the results may be a bit mushy.

10. **HOW TO REHEAT FOOD SAFELY** Regardless of what ingredients a dish contains, how you thaw it or even whether it was frozen or not, once you've reheated it to 165°F (75°C), the food is safe to consume.

Your Kitchen

1. **YOUR PREP ZONE** Set yourself up for success by organizing the area around your stove and prep area. Neatly arrange all the various tools and ingredients that you use frequently: salt, pepper, cooking oils, kitchen towels, utensils and anything else you regularly need.

2. **READ THE RECIPE** Read the recipe all the way through, then gather everything you need to make it—ingredients and utensils—before beginning. Use a book stand or heavy-duty binder clips to keep your cookbooks visible but away from any mess.

3. **ORGANIZING TRAY** Use baking sheets or platters to contain and organize your raw ingredients and tools. This will enhance your efficiency and prevent clutter that can lead to messy mistakes.

4. **RECEIVING AND DISCARD BOWLS** Pros know that work surfaces are not for storing food or waste. Instead, they use a series of small containers to hold prepped ingredients and their inevitable waste. As you prep, don't let peelings, cores and scraps accumulate. Have a vessel ready to contain the mess.

5. **TASTING SPOONS** You can learn lots about cooking if you taste every chance you get, so be prepared to taste as you go. Set up a container of small tasting spoons so you're poised to taste each step of the way.

6. **SLOW COOKER** A reliable slow cooker is one of the great time-saving devices of any kitchen. There are so many meals that can be simply started in one and forgotten for the day. Fill it with flavor and walk away knowing that when you return, dinner is seconds from being served.

7. **STORAGE BAGS AND CONTAINERS** Plan ahead and have on hand an array of heavy-duty zip-top plastic bags and containers ready to receive prepped food and leftovers for long-term storage.

8. **CLEAN AS YOU GO** Nothing is more inefficient or demoralizing than a pile of dirty dishes to tackle when you're done cooking. Fill a sink with hot soapy water and wash as you go. Fill a small tub or vessel with water and toss in tools that need a quick soaking.

9. **HANDLING RAW MEAT** Be sure to handle these ingredients with tongs instead of your bare hands, and don't place them on any work surfaces at all. To cut down on the chance of cross-contamination, use a simple plate to hold the prepped meat or fish—it's rinsed and cleaned much more easily than a larger cutting board. If you need to cut the ingredient, many cooks prefer to keep a second cutting board strictly for use with raw meat and fish.

10. **CUT DOWN ON CLUTTER** Use small baskets or other containers to group and organize similar tools or ingredients. This can significantly improve the look of open shelves while making it a lot easier for you to find what you're looking for.

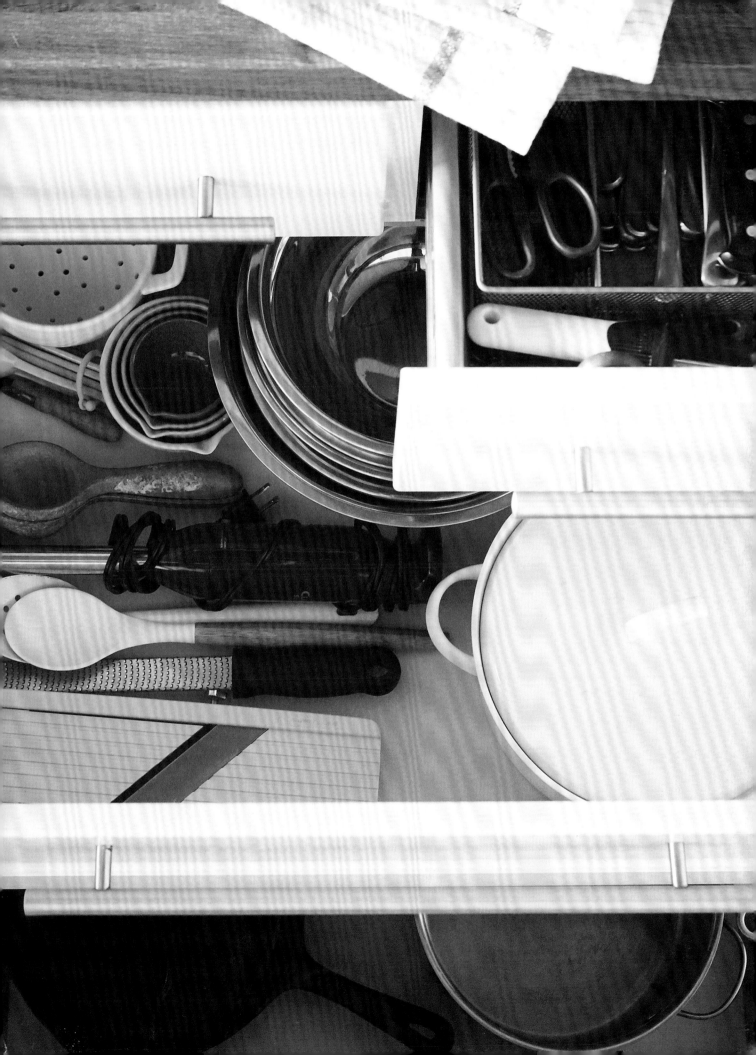

BREAKFAST AND DAY BAKING

BREAKFAST AND DAY BAKING RECIPES

BAKED WESTERN OMELET

This classic group of flavors tastes great any day of the week, especially when you've baked it ahead to help you quickly kick-start your day. Cook ahead so when the time comes, you can get your day going in a hurry.

MAKES 6 OR 8 SLICES, EASILY DOUBLED IN 2 BATCHES USING SAME PAN

TODAY FOR TOMORROW   Prep the ham and vegetables a few days in advance, ready to cook. Refrigerate tightly sealed in a zip-top bag. • Fully cook this dish now and reheat anytime during the next several days (see Storage Tip).

Preheat your oven to 350°F (180°C). Turn on your convection fan if you have one.

Toss the ham, bell peppers and a splash of vegetable oil into a large ovenproof nonstick skillet over medium-high heat. Sauté them until they sizzle, soften and smell delicious, 3 to 5 minutes. Meanwhile, in a large bowl, whisk together the eggs, then whisk in the milk, cheese, green onions, salt and pepper.

When the peppers are ready, pour the egg mixture into the pan and stir gently until large curds form and at least half of the egg is cooked, 2 or 3 minutes. Place the pan in the oven and bake until the omelet is firm, 10 to 15 minutes. Serve from the pan or carefully invert the omelet onto a serving plate.

6 to 8 thin slices of deli ham, chopped

1 red bell pepper, diced

1 green bell pepper, diced

A splash of vegetable oil

12 eggs

½ cup (125 mL) of milk

2 cups (500 mL) of grated cheddar cheese

4 green onions, thinly sliced

¼ teaspoon (1 mL) of salt

Lots of freshly ground pepper

STORAGE TIP

Refrigerate: Tightly seal the cooked omelet and refrigerate within 30 minutes of cooking. Store for up to 4 days before reheating.

Freeze: Portion, tightly seal and freeze for up to 30 days. Thaw in the refrigerator for 1 or 2 days before reheating. Tightly seal leftovers and store in the refrigerator for just a few days.

TORTILLA QUICHES

Here's a big burst of bright flavor to begin your day—spicy salsa, smoky cumin and aromatic cilantro in a crispy, cheesy egg cup. And these Tex-Mex treats are a savory way to start every day when you've got a batch baked and ready. MAKES 6 MINI QUICHES, EASILY DOUBLED

TODAY FOR TOMORROW Prep the vegetables a day or two in advance, ready to cook when the time comes. Refrigerate tightly sealed in a zip-top bag • Prepare (but don't bake) a batch of these mini quiches, refrigerate overnight, and bake in the morning. If you're baking straight from the fridge, add a few minutes to the cooking time. • Fully cook this dish now and reheat anytime during the next several days. Baked quiches can also be refrigerated or frozen (see Storage Tip).

6 medium flour tortillas

18 cherry tomatoes, each cut in half

2 green onions, thinly sliced

A large handful of fresh cilantro leaves, lightly chopped

8 eggs

1 cup (250 mL) of your favorite salsa

1 teaspoon (5 mL) of ground cumin

1 cup (250 mL) of grated cheddar cheese

Preheat your oven to 350°F (180°C). Turn on your convection fan if you have one. Lightly spray a muffin pan with extra-large cups with cooking spray. Set the muffin pan on a baking sheet to contain any drips.

Wrap the tortillas in a damp paper towel and microwave them until they're soft and pliable, 30 seconds or so. Line each muffin cup with the tortillas, pleating and folding them to fit.

Stir together the tomatoes, green onions and cilantro. Divide the fragrant mixture evenly among the tortillas. Whisk together the eggs, salsa, cumin and half of the cheese. Divide the mixture evenly among the muffin cups. Top with the remaining cheese. Bake until the quiches are firm to the touch, nearly cooked through but still slightly moist on top, 25 to 30 minutes. Rest for 5 minutes or so as they finish firming before serving.

STORAGE TIP

Refrigerate: Tightly seal the baked quiches and refrigerate within 30 minutes of cooking. Store for up to 4 days.

Freeze: Tightly seal the baked quiches and freeze for up to 30 days. Reheat straight from frozen or thaw in the refrigerator for 1 to 2 days before reheating. Tightly seal leftovers and store in the refrigerator for just a few days.

POTATO BACON CHEDDAR SKILLET

You can't beat potatoes, bacon and cheddar in any dish, and this one is such a great way to use up leftover baked potatoes that you just might find yourself baking extra with breakfast in mind! It's so easy to toss a few extra potatoes into the oven next time you're baking a batch to have with dinner.   MAKES 1 SKILLET, SERVES 2 TO 4, EASILY DOUBLED IN 2 BATCHES USING SAME PAN

TODAY FOR TOMORROW   Bake the potatoes a few days in advance. Refrigerate tightly sealed in a zip-top bag • Fully cook this dish now and reheat anytime during the next several days (see Storage Tip).

4 thick slices of bacon,
  cut into thin strips

2 or 3 large baked potatoes,
  cut into large chunks

¼ teaspoon (1 mL) of salt

Lots of freshly ground pepper

4 eggs

½ cup (125 mL) of grated
  cheddar cheese

2 or 3 green onions, thinly sliced

Toss the bacon and a big splash of water into a large nonstick skillet over medium-high heat. Cook until the bacon is fully browned and evenly crispy, 10 minutes or so. Strain out the bacon, leaving the flavorful fat behind. Add the potatoes, season with salt and pepper and toss to evenly coat. Fry the potatoes, turning frequently, until evenly browned and crispy, about 15 minutes.

Meanwhile, whisk together the eggs, cheese, green onions and crispy bacon bits. When the potatoes are done, reduce the heat to medium, pour off some of the fat and gently stir in the eggs. Continue stirring until half or so of the egg mixture is cooked. Cover with a lid and cook until the eggs are firm, 2 or 3 minutes.

STORAGE TIP

Refrigerate: Tightly seal the skillet and refrigerate within 30 minutes of cooking. Store for up to 3 days before reheating.

MORNING GRANOLA

We all know how essential great breakfasts are for the whole family, so don't let anything get in the way of a day's worth of whole-grain goodness. Make a batch or two of your own granola and you'll be set for the week. This incredibly delicious granola is far superior to store-bought cereal and extremely easy to make ahead of busy breakfast time. It's a perfect weekend project. MAKES 15 CUPS (3.5 L), 12 SERVINGS, EASILY DOUBLED

TODAY FOR TOMORROW   Mix the ingredients a few days in advance, ready to bake when the time comes. Store tightly sealed in a zip-top bag. • Bake this granola now and enjoy for the next week or so (see Storage Tip).

Preheat your oven to 325°F (160°C). Turn on your convection fan if you have one. Line 2 baking sheets with parchment paper or foil and spray with a light film of cooking spray.

Measure the oil, honey, cinnamon, nutmeg and vanilla into a small saucepan. Whisk gently over medium heat until the honey melts into the oil and the spices release their flavors, 2 or 3 minutes.

Toss the oats into a large bowl, then pour the aromatic honey over them. Stir until everything is thoroughly combined. Divide the mixture between the baking sheets, spreading it into an even layer. (Don't wash the bowl.) Bake, stirring every 10 minutes or so to ensure even browning, for about 40 minutes or until the granola is golden brown and fragrant.

In the same bowl, stir together the almonds, raisins, sunflower seeds and pumpkin seeds. Carefully scrape the hot granola into the bowl, then toss the works together. Pour back onto the baking sheets to cool before storing.

1 cup (250 mL) of any vegetable oil

1 cup (250 mL) of honey

1 tablespoon (15 mL) or so of cinnamon

1 tablespoon (15 mL) or so of nutmeg

1 tablespoon (15 mL) of pure vanilla extract

8 cups (2 L) of any oats (instant, large-flake or steel-cut)

3 cups (750 mL) of almonds or your favorite nuts

2 cups (500 mL) of raisins or your favorite dried fruit

1 cup (250 mL) of sunflower seeds

1 cup (250 mL) of pumpkin seeds

STORAGE TIP

Room Temperature: Cool the granola, tightly seal and store for up to 10 days.

GRANOLA BARS

Need a little mid-morning or mid-afternoon boost? Skip the candy aisle and instead stir whole-grain goodness into a batch of these super-simple, super-tasty granola bars. Artfully wrap and tie individual bars for some added flair—and lovingly tuck a handwritten note inside.   MAKES 16 GRANOLA BARS, EASILY DOUBLED IN 2 PANS

TODAY FOR TOMORROW   Make the granola a few days in advance, ready to bake into bars when the time comes. Tightly seal in a zip-top bag. • Make these granola bars ahead and enjoy for the next week or so (see Storage Tip).

2 cups (500 mL) of granola
   (page 11)
2 cups (500 mL) of instant
   rolled oats
1 cup (250 mL) of brown sugar
½ cup (125 mL) of your favorite nuts,
   seeds or dried fruit
½ cup (125 mL) of water
1 teaspoon (5 mL) of cinnamon or
   your favorite baking spice

Preheat your oven to 350°F (180°C). Turn on your convection fan if you have one. Line an 8-inch (2 L) square baking pan with foil and spray with a light film of cooking spray.

Mix everything together in a large bowl, then evenly spread into the pan, pressing and compacting the mixture as firmly as possible. For best results, place an identical or slightly smaller pan inside and press down with all your weight. Bake until lightly browned and very firm to the touch, 20 minutes or so, then rest until cool. Remove from the pan, slice the bars and wrap individually in plastic wrap or bags.

STORAGE TIP

Room Temperature: Cool the granola bars, tightly seal in a zip-top bag and store for up to 10 days.

Freeze: Cool, tightly seal and freeze for up to a month.

AMAZING MORNING MICROWAVE MUFFINS

Craving fresh-baked goodness in a hurry? This kitchen hack will impress everyone. And it's the perfect treat to pack for work. Just measure the dry mix and stir-ins into a mason jar along with the butter and an egg nestled in for the ride. When you're ready for a muffin, crack the egg into the works and stir together thoroughly. Experiment with different spices in the base mix; you can even add a spoonful of cocoa powder or chocolate chips. MAKES 12 MUFFINS, EASILY DOUBLED

TODAY FOR TOMORROW   Make the dry-mix base ahead (see Storage Tip). The muffins are best enjoyed as soon as you make them.

FOR THE DRY-MIX BASE

3 cups (750 mL) of all-purpose flour

½ cup (125 mL) of brown sugar

¼ cup (60 mL) of baking powder

1 tablespoon (15 mL) of nutmeg
  or your favorite baking spice

FOR EACH MUFFIN

¼ cup (60 mL) of the dry-mix base

¼ cup (60 mL) of your favorite
  stir-ins: any nuts, seeds, dried
  or fresh fruit

1 teaspoon (5 mL) of butter,
  softened or melted

1 egg

For the dry-mix base, whisk together the flour, sugar, baking powder and nutmeg.

Whenever you feel like a freshly baked muffin, in a standard coffee mug or a 1-cup (250 mL) wide-mouth mason jar, combine the dry mix, your choice of stir-ins, the butter and a freshly cracked egg. Stir well. Microwave for 1 minute. Turn out and enjoy with the freshest cup of coffee you can find.

STORAGE TIP

Room Temperature: Tightly seal and store the dry mix for up to 30 days.

FRUIT MUFFINS

If you're going to bake muffins, you might as well bake amazing muffins. These ones stay delicious for days because the oil in the batter helps keep them moist. The variety of ingredients you can use is endless, so you'll never get bored with these easy muffins. Blueberries work very well, as do raspberries and blackberries or finely chopped apples, pears, peaches, mangoes or bananas. These are a perfect weekend baking project.
MAKES 12 LARGE OR 24 REGULAR MUFFINS, EASILY DOUBLED

TODAY FOR TOMORROW   Measure and prep the dry and wet ingredients separately a day or two in advance, ready to combine and bake when the time comes. • Bake these muffins ahead (see Storage Tip).

FOR THE CRUMBLE TOPPING

1 cup (250 mL) of brown sugar

½ cup (125 mL) of all-purpose flour

½ teaspoon (2 mL) of cinnamon

¼ cup (60 mL) of butter, softened

FOR THE MUFFIN BATTER

4½ cups (1.125 L) of all-purpose flour

2¼ cups (550 mL) of sugar

2 tablespoons (30 mL) of baking powder

1 tablespoon (15 mL) of nutmeg

1½ teaspoons (7 mL) of salt

3 cups (750 mL) of your favorite fresh or frozen fruit, finely chopped if need be

3 eggs

2½ cups (625 mL) of milk

1 cup (250 mL) of vegetable oil or melted butter

1 tablespoon (15 mL) of pure vanilla extract

Preheat your oven to 350°F (180°C). Turn on your convection fan if you have one. Lightly oil your muffin pan with cooking spray.

Make the crumble first. Whisk together the brown sugar, flour and cinnamon. Rub the butter into the mixture with your fingers until evenly mixed and crumbly. Set aside.

Make the muffin batter next. In a large bowl, whisk together the flour, sugar, baking powder, nutmeg and salt. In a separate bowl, toss your fruit choice with a few spoonfuls of the flour mixture. This helps keep the fruit from sinking to the bottom of the muffins. Crack the eggs into a large measuring cup and add enough milk to make 3 cups (750 mL) of liquid. Whisk the oil and vanilla into the egg mixture, then add all the liquids to the dry ingredients. Switch to a wooden spoon and with a few quick, deliberate strokes, stir the works just until barely combined, taking care not to overmix and toughen the batter. Gently stir in the fruit.

Carefully fill each muffin cup to the rim. Generously sprinkle the crumble topping evenly on top of each muffin. Bake for 25 minutes or so for larger muffins or 20 minutes or so for the regular size. The muffins are done when a toothpick poked into the center comes out clean. Turn out onto racks to cool.

STORAGE TIP

Room Temperature: Cool the muffins completely, tightly seal in a zip-top bag and store for up to 4 days.

Refrigerate: Tightly seal and refrigerate for up to a week.

Freeze: Tightly seal and freeze for up to 30 days. Thaw, sealed, at room temperature for an hour or so. (Ovens and microwaves tend to dry and toughen muffins.)

BLUEBERRY SOUR CREAM COFFEE CAKE

Coffee cake is easy to make—and easier to enjoy. A good one is moist and delicious, but a spectacular one is covered with a thick, buttery streusel and layered with moist blueberries. Planning breakfast or brunch? A bake sale or holidays on the horizon? This delicious coffee cake is perfect for so many occasions. MAKES 16 TO 20 PIECES, EASILY DOUBLED IN 2 PANS

TODAY FOR TOMORROW Combine the cake's dry ingredients a few days in advance, ready to bake when the time comes. Store tightly sealed in a zip-top bag. • Prepare the streusel topping a few days in advance. Store tightly sealed in a zip-top bag. • Bake this coffee cake ahead (see Storage Tip).

Preheat your oven to 350°F (180°C). Turn on your convection fan if you have one. Lightly oil a 13- × 9-inch (3.5 L) baking pan.

Make the streusel topping first. Whisk together the brown sugar, flour and cinnamon. Rub the butter into the mixture with your fingers until evenly mixed and crumbly. Set aside.

Make the batter. In a large bowl, whisk together the flour, sugar, baking powder, baking soda and salt. In a separate bowl, whisk together the eggs, then whisk in the sour cream and lemon zest. Add the wet ingredients to the dry, switch to a wooden spoon and with a few quick, deliberate strokes, stir the works just until barely combined, taking care not to overmix and toughen the batter.

Spread half the batter into the prepared pan, then cover evenly with the blueberries. Top with the remaining batter, smoothing the top. Sprinkle with a thick layer of the streusel topping. Bake until a skewer inserted in the center comes out clean, about 1 hour. Cool before slicing.

STORAGE TIP

Room Temperature: Cool the coffee cake completely, tightly seal in a zip-top bag and store for up to 4 days.

Freeze: Portion, tightly seal and freeze for up to 30 days. Thaw, sealed, at room temperature for a couple of hours. (Ovens and microwaves tend to dry and toughen cake.)

FOR THE STREUSEL TOPPING

1 cup (250 mL) of brown sugar

1 cup (250 mL) of all-purpose flour

2 tablespoons (30 mL) of cinnamon

½ cup (125 mL) of butter, diced into small pieces and softened

FOR THE CAKE BATTER

3 cups (750 mL) of all-purpose flour

2 cups (500 mL) of sugar

4 teaspoons (20 mL) of baking powder

1 teaspoon (5 mL) of baking soda

½ teaspoon (2 mL) of salt

4 eggs

2 cups (500 mL) of sour cream

The zest of 2 or 3 lemons

2 cups (500 mL) of fresh or frozen blueberries

EVERYDAY WHOLE-GRAIN BREAD

Some things can't be rushed and must be made ahead. Good bread is one of them. Old-fashioned bread dough wasn't made with machines or long, tedious kneading. It was made with knowledge of Mother Nature's patient ability to create a naturally elastic dough from no more than flour, water, yeast and time. Time for long, stretchy gluten strands to magically form all by themselves. Golden brown goodness from plain white blandness!

It's just as easy to make several loaves as it is to make one, so try a weekend baking rally to be ready for the weeks ahead. If you're making more than one loaf, for accuracy measure out and make each one separately.

MAKES 1 LARGE LOAF, EASY TO MAKE 2 OR 3 AT THE SAME TIME

TODAY FOR TOMORROW Measure the dry ingredients a few days in advance, ready to bake when the time comes. Store tightly sealed in a zip-top bag. • Bake this bread ahead (see Storage Tip).

3 cups (750 mL) of all-purpose or bread flour

1 cup (250 mL) of Red Fife or other whole wheat flour

½ cup (125 mL) of any multi-grain blend for hot cereal such as Red River Cereal

1 teaspoon (5 mL) of salt

Heaping ½ teaspoon (3 mL) of active dry yeast

2¼ cups (550 mL) of warm water

In a large bowl, whisk together the all-purpose flour, whole wheat flour, multi-grain blend, salt and yeast. Measure in the water, and with the handle of a wooden spoon, vigorously stir until a coarse, wet dough forms, just a minute or two. Continue stirring with the handle until all the flour is gathered up into an evenly mixed yet still moist dough ball, a few minutes more.

Cover the bowl with drum-tight plastic wrap and rest overnight on your kitchen counter. In 8 hours or so, a strong, elastic dough will have formed and risen.

Preheat your oven to 425°F (220°C). Turn on your convection fan if you have one. Lightly oil a large loaf pan.

Gather the dough from the edge and flip it over, deflating it. Lightly flour the surface and roll and knead as best you can into a tight ball, adding more flour as needed. Transfer it to the loaf pan and encourage it into the corners. Rest, uncovered, until the dough doubles in size and rises above the rim of the pan, an hour or two. Gently place in the oven and bake until it pulls slightly away from the sides of the pan and is evenly browned and crusty, 45 to 50 minutes. If you like, insert an instant-read thermometer into the bread—you'll know it's done when it reaches 195°F (90°C). Immediately remove the loaf from the pan. Rest until it's cool enough to handle before slicing.

STORAGE TIP

Room Temperature: Cool the bread completely, tightly seal in a zip-top bag and store for up to 4 days.

Freeze: Tightly seal and freeze for up to 30 days. Thaw, sealed, for an hour or so at room temperature. (Ovens and microwaves tend to dry and toughen bread.)

MONKEY BREAD
AND BANANA BUTTER

The only thing better than tearing your own little steaming cinnamon-scented roll off a loaf and slathering it with delicious banana butter is watching your family and friends do the same thing before showering the baker with thanks and praise. Monkey bread is the perfect weekend morning treat—and so easy when you bake a batch the day before and gently warm it. MAKES A 13- × 9-INCH (3.5 L) PAN, 15 OR 24 PIECES

TODAY FOR TOMORROW Measure the dry ingredients a few days in advance, ready to bake when the time comes. Store tightly sealed in a zip-top bag. • Make and shape the dough the night before, refrigerate overnight, then rest at room temperature for 30 minutes or so before baking the next morning. • Bake this bread ahead (see Storage Tip).

Begin with the dough. Measure the milk, brown sugar, melted butter, yeast and vanilla into the bowl of a stand mixer. Stir together with the dough hook just long enough to dissolve the sugar, not even a minute. Add the flour and salt and continue kneading on low speed until a smooth, elastic dough forms and then pulls away from the side of the bowl, about 5 minutes. Transfer the dough to a lightly oiled bowl and cover drum-tight with plastic wrap. Rest the dough on your kitchen counter until it doubles in size, 2 to 3 hours.

Pour the melted butter for rolling the dough into a large, shallow dish. In another shallow dish, whisk together the sugar and cinnamon. Lightly oil a 13- × 9-inch (3.5 L) baking pan.

Knock down the risen dough and pull and tug it into 15 or 24 equal pieces. Roll each piece under your palm until it forms into a tight ball. (You may find it helpful to lightly moisten the rolling surface with a drop or two of water.) Roll each ball in the melted butter, coating it thoroughly and draining well, then neatly roll in the cinnamon sugar. If you've made 15 balls, arrange them 3 × 5 in the pan, or 6 × 4 for 24 balls. Rest, uncovered, until doubled in size, an hour or so.

Meanwhile, preheat your oven to 350°F (180°C). Turn on your convection fan if you have one. Carefully place the risen dough in the oven and bake until golden brown, 30 to 40 minutes. Serve warm.

You can make the banana butter while you're waiting for the dough to rise or while the bread bakes. Mash the bananas, butter, honey and vanilla with a fork or spoon, or for a really smooth consistency, blend in a blender or food processor. Fill a small festive bowl with the butter ready to spread on the freshly baked, freshly torn monkey bread balls.

FOR THE DOUGH

2 cups (500 mL) of milk

¼ cup (60 mL) of brown sugar

¼ cup (60 mL) of butter, melted

1 tablespoon (15 mL) of instant yeast

1 tablespoon (15 mL) of pure
  vanilla extract

5 cups (1.25 L) of all-purpose flour

1 teaspoon (5 mL) of salt

TO ROLL THE DOUGH

½ cup (125 mL) of butter, melted

1 cup (250 mL) of sugar

3 tablespoons (45 mL) of cinnamon

FOR THE BANANA BUTTER

2 ripe bananas

½ cup (125 mL) of butter, softened

2 tablespoons (30 mL) of honey

½ teaspoon (2 mL) of pure
  vanilla extract

STORAGE TIP

Room Temperature: Tightly seal the bread and refrigerate for up to 6 days. • Refrigerate the butter for a week or so.

Freeze: Tightly seal the bread and freeze for up to 30 days. Thaw, sealed, for an hour or two at room temperature. (Ovens and microwaves tend to dry and toughen bread.) • Tightly seal and freeze the butter for a month or more.

SNACKS, STARTERS AND SALADS

SNACKS, STARTERS AND SALADS RECIPES

BUTTERY BUTTERSCOTCH POPCORN

It's okay to show off in the kitchen now and then. When the urge strikes, a batch of butterscotch-flavored freshly popped popcorn is a great showstopper snack—especially when you pop the popcorn in lots of butter. Double the batch to make enough for a week's worth of whole-grain lunchbox treats. It's not junk food if it's homemade! MAKES 4 OR 5 QUARTS (4 OR 5 L), EASILY DOUBLED IN A LARGER POT OR MAKE 2 BATCHES OF POPCORN ONE RIGHT AFTER THE OTHER. THE BUTTERSCOTCH CAN BE DOUBLED IN ONE LARGER POT.

TODAY FOR TOMORROW Make the butterscotch a few days in advance and store in the refrigerator in a tightly sealed container for up to 2 weeks. Reheat in the microwave or in a glass jar set in a saucepan of simmering water. Heat until the butterscotch has returned to its original consistency before tossing with the popcorn. • Make this popcorn dish now and enjoy over the next week (see Storage Tip).

Position oven racks slightly above and below the middle and preheat your oven to 275°F (140°C). Turn on your convection fan if you have one. Line 2 baking sheets with parchment paper or foil and lightly oil the paper or foil.

Match a large pot with a tight-fitting lid and set it over medium-high heat. Toss in the butter (it seems like a lot, but every tasty drop will be absorbed). Swirl the butter gently as it melts, foams and eventually browns and forms flavorful sediment. Take the tasty brown bits as far as you dare, but don't let them blacken. Immediately add the popcorn and gently shake and shiver it into an even layer. Quickly grind in lots of pepper, lots.

Listen and watch until a few kernels pop and escape from the pot. Cover the pot, leaving the lid slightly askew to vent the steam. Listen carefully. The tempo of the popping will increase from sporadic to constant. When it seems to slow, tighten the lid and turn off the heat. When the crescendo dissipates, pour the popcorn into the largest bowl you can find, making sure to discard any unpopped kernels.

Make the butterscotch. Pour the water into a medium saucepan over medium-high heat. Pour the sugar into a small island in the middle of the sea. Don't stir! The water and sugar will quickly dissolve together and form smooth simple syrup. When you see the first hint of golden brown, begin gently swirling the pan for even coloring. When the sugar is as deep golden brown as you dare, turn off the heat, add the butter all at once and carefully whisk until it's smoothly incorporated.

Working quickly, evenly drizzle the butterscotch over the popcorn, tossing and adding until they're thoroughly mixed. Spread the works out on the baking sheets and bake, without stirring, until the popcorn dries and crisps, about 20 minutes. Rest until cool enough to handle.

STORAGE TIP

Room Temperature: Cool the popcorn, tightly seal in bags or containers and store for up to 7 days.

FOR THE POPCORN

½ pound (225 g) or so of salted butter

1 cup (250 mL) of plain popping corn

Lots of freshly ground pepper but no salt—there's plenty in the butter

FOR THE BUTTERSCOTCH

1 cup (250 mL) of water

1 cup (250 mL) of sugar

½ cup (125 mL) of cold butter, cut into small cubes

PUMPKIN PIE SEEDS

Snacking is an important part of life, even a healthy, homemade part of life. Best of all, snacks can easily be made far in advance so you can skip straight to tasty when the urge strikes. A handful of spicy pumpkin seeds is a super place to start. Pumpkin seeds are not only full of fiber but they readily soak up this salty, spicy, snacky goodness. MAKES 4 CUPS (1 L), EASILY DOUBLED

TODAY FOR TOMORROW Simmer the seeds a few days in advance and leave to soak in their brine, ready to strain and bake when the time comes (see Storage Tip).

Preheat your oven to 350°F (180°C). Turn on your convection fan if you have one. Line a baking sheet with parchment paper or foil and lightly oil the paper or foil.

Measure everything except the pumpkin seeds into a small saucepan and bring to a slow, steady simmer for a few minutes. Stir in the pumpkin seeds and simmer for a few minutes so they soften. Turn off the heat and rest long enough for the flavors to absorb, at least 15 minutes.

Strain the seeds, reserving the reusable liquid. Spread them evenly on the prepared pan. Bake, without stirring, until lightly crisped and browned, 15 to 20 minutes. As they cool, they'll crisp further.

STORAGE TIP

Room Temperature: Cool the seeds, tightly seal in a zip-top bag and store for up to 10 days.

4 cups (1 L) of water

1 cup (250 mL) of brown sugar

¼ cup (60 mL) of Sriracha or your favorite hot sauce

2 tablespoons (30 mL) of salt

2 tablespoons (30 mL) of ground ginger

1 tablespoon (15 mL) of ground allspice

1 tablespoon (15 mL) of cinnamon

1 tablespoon (15 mL) of nutmeg

1 teaspoon (5 mL) of ground cloves

4 cups (1 L) of unsalted raw pumpkin seeds

SMASHED JALAPEÑO MINT GUACAMOLE WITH CHERRY TOMATOES

There are so many ways to make guacamole! This authentically rustic version is literally smashed together for simplicity and flavor. It's flavored with spicy hot jalapeño tempered with cooling mint. The surface of guacamole will oxidize and brown as it rests, so press a piece of plastic wrap directly onto the surface to keep out air. MAKES 4 CUPS (1 L), EASILY DOUBLED OR TRIPLED

TODAY FOR TOMORROW Make this guacamole ahead (see Storage Tip).

Crush the garlic cloves under the side of your knife blade before mincing them relentlessly with the jalapeños. Add the salt for an abrasive effect. When you can't mince any finer, smear the works into a paste under the side of your blade.

In a large bowl, stir the garlic paste with the mint, lime zest and lime juice. Halve the avocados and scoop their flesh into the bowl, mashing and smashing with a fork as you go. Stir in the tomatoes. Mound the proceeds into a festive dipping bowl and surround with crunchy chips, crackers or veggie dippers.

STORAGE TIP

Refrigerate: Tightly seal and refrigerate for up to 6 days.

Freeze: Tightly seal and freeze for up to 30 days. Thaw in the refrigerator for 1 or 2 days. Tightly seal leftovers and store in the refrigerator for just a few days.

2 garlic cloves

2 jalapeño peppers, seeds removed

1 teaspoon (5 mL) of salt

Leaves from 1 large bunch of fresh mint (12 sprigs or so), finely chopped

The zest and juice of 2 limes

4 avocados

1 pint (500 mL) of cherry tomatoes, halved

Chips, crackers or veggie dippers

CURRIED CARROT HUMMUS

Hummus is perhaps the world's greatest dip. It's unparalleled for addictive flavor, smooth texture, nutritional value and the all-important functionality factor. With a batch of hummus ready, you can really release your creative juices. Try it on your favorite crackers, flatbreads or chips. Then top with smoked salmon, various charcuterie, even just plain sprinkled with green onions or giant dill sprigs. MAKES 2½ CUPS (625 ML), EASILY DOUBLED OR TRIPLED

TODAY FOR TOMORROW   Prepare this dish a few days in advance, ready to serve when the time comes (see Storage Tip).

1 tablespoon (15 mL) of cumin seeds

1 tablespoon (15 mL) of coriander seeds

2 large carrots, grated

2 garlic cloves, smashed

1 cup (250 mL) of orange juice

1 tablespoon (15 mL) of curry powder

½ teaspoon (2 mL) of salt

A 19-ounce (540 mL) can of chickpeas, drained and well rinsed

½ cup (125 mL) of tahini

¼ cup (60 mL) of your very best olive oil

1 teaspoon (5 mL) or more of your favorite hot sauce

The zest and juice of 1 lemon

A mess of vegetables, crackers, chips or other dippers

Gently toast the cumin and coriander seeds in a small dry pot over medium heat, shaking and shivering until lightly toasted and deliciously fragrant, 2 or 3 minutes. Add the carrots, garlic, orange juice, curry powder and salt. Bring to a simmer, cover and cook until the carrots are tender, about 15 minutes.

Carefully pour the hot mixture into a blender or food processor. Add the chickpeas, tahini, olive oil, hot sauce, and lemon zest and juice. Blend until smooth. Add a splash or two or more of water if you prefer a thinner consistency or to get the works going. Smooth into a festive bowl and serve with veggies or other dippers.

STORAGE TIP

Refrigerate: Tightly seal and refrigerate for up to 7 days.

Freeze: Tightly seal and freeze for up to 30 days. Thaw in the refrigerator for 1 or 2 days. Tightly seal leftovers and store in the refrigerator for just a few days.

BLACK OLIVE
BABA GHANOUSH AND
MINI PITA CHIPS

Something mysterious yet addictive happens when you blend smooth, slightly bitter eggplant with aromatic, slightly bitter black olives and rich, slightly bitter tahini. The secret is the sour, spicy, salty and savory notes that balance the bitter. Or maybe it's the irresistible crunch of the crispy pitas. Either way, a batch of this dip in your refrigerator is like money in the bank. With it you can inspire a week's worth of daily dipping. Spread it on flatbread and top with a charcuterie or vegetable garnish.   MAKES 3 TO 4 CUPS (750 ML TO 1 L) OF BABA GHANOUSH AND 48 MINI PITAS, EASILY DOUBLED

TODAY FOR TOMORROW   Make this dip ahead (see Storage Tip). ● Crisp the pitas a few days in advance, ready to dip when the time comes (see Storage Tip).

Preheat your oven to 350°F (180°C). Turn on your convection fan if you have one. Line a baking sheet with parchment paper or foil.

Crisp the pitas first. Spread them out on the baking sheet. Stir together the oil and honey and brush evenly on the pitas. Sprinkle them with seeds and season with salt and pepper. Bake until evenly golden brown and thoroughly crispy, 15 to 20 minutes. Rest and cool.

Turn the oven up to 400°F (200°C). Brush the cut side of each eggplant half with a generous spoonful of olive oil and arrange cut side up on the baking sheet.

Cut two 6-inch (15 cm) squares of foil. Place a head of garlic in the middle of each and drizzle with some olive oil. Wrap the foil tightly around the head and nestle in with the eggplant. Bake until the eggplants collapse and are completely translucent and tender, almost creamy, 40 to 50 minutes or so.

When the eggplant is cool enough to handle, toss it, skin and all, into your food processor. Squeeze the garlic like toothpaste onto the eggplant. Add the lemon zest and juice, tahini, Sriracha and salt. Process until smooth. Add the olives and briefly pulse just enough to coarsely chop them, maybe 5 pulses. Spoon into a serving bowl and garnish with whole olives, another drizzle of olive oil and a few pinches of paprika.

STORAGE TIP

Room Temperature: Tightly seal the pitas and store for up to a week.

Refrigerate: Tightly seal the dip and refrigerate for up to 6 days.

Freeze: Tightly seal the dip and freeze for up to 30 days. Thaw in the refrigerator for 1 or 2 days. Tightly seal leftovers and store in the refrigerator for just a few days.

FOR THE MINI PITAS

48 mini pitas (or 8 regular pitas, stacked and sliced into 6 wedges each)

1 tablespoon (15 mL) of extra virgin olive oil

1 tablespoon (15 mL) of honey

2 tablespoons (30 mL) of sesame seeds or poppy seeds

Sprinkles of salt, preferably a flaky type

Lots of freshly ground pepper

FOR THE BABA GHANOUSH

2 eggplants, each end trimmed, cut in half lengthwise

¼ cup (60 mL) of extra virgin olive oil

2 whole heads of garlic with their tops cut off

The zest and juice of 1 lemon

¼ cup (60 mL) of tahini

½ teaspoon (2 mL) of Sriracha or your favorite hot sauce

½ teaspoon (2 mL) of salt

1 cup (250 mL) of Kalamata olives, pitted (reserve a few for garnishing)

A few pinches of paprika

REALLY GOOD FOCACCIA
WITH DRIED-TOMATO BUTTER

My family enjoys tugging and tearing a freshly baked focaccia to bits, then smothering it with bright, tasty tomato butter. I enjoy making the dough, knowing that Mother Nature does most of the work for me. No kneading, just easy stirring and patient resting, which makes it too easy to bake ahead and freeze.

MAKES 1 LARGE FOCACCIA, 12 LARGE SLICES, EASILY DOUBLED OR TRIPLED (FOR ACCURACY, MEASURE AND MAKE EACH BATCH SEPARATELY)

TODAY FOR TOMORROW   Make the tomato butter ahead (see Storage Tip). • Make the dough the night before or the morning of, and rest for 8 to 10 hours before baking. • Bake the focaccia and store at room temperature, refrigerate or freeze (see Storage Tip).

FOR THE FOCACCIA DOUGH

2 tablespoons (30 mL) of extra virgin olive oil

1 large onion, finely chopped

4 garlic cloves, minced

Leaves from 2 to 3 sprigs of fresh rosemary, lightly chopped

5 cups (1.25 L) of all-purpose flour

2 teaspoons (10 mL) of fine salt

Heaping ½ teaspoon (3 mL) of active dry yeast

1 cup (250 mL) of grated Parmigiano-Reggiano cheese

1 cup (250 mL) of Kalamata olives, pitted and halved

2½ cups (625 mL) of warm water

FOR THE FINISHED DOUGH

Leaves from 1 sprig of fresh rosemary, lightly chopped

1 or 2 ripe tomatoes, thinly sliced

½ teaspoon (2 mL) of coarse flaky salt

Lots of freshly ground pepper

FOR THE DRIED TOMATO BUTTER

16 oil-packed sun-dried tomatoes

½ cup (125 mL) of butter, softened

1 tablespoon (15 mL) of dried oregano

2 handfuls of fresh parsley, chopped

Lots of freshly ground pepper

Begin with the dough. Splash the olive oil into a small sauté pan over medium-high heat. Toss in the onion and garlic and sauté until lightly browned and fragrant, about 5 minutes. Turn off the heat and toss in the rosemary.

Measure the flour, salt and yeast into a large bowl and whisk them together. Stir in the Parmesan and olives, then the onion mixture. Measure in the water, and with the handle of a wooden spoon, vigorously stir until a coarse dough forms, just a minute or two. Continue stirring with the handle until all the flour is gathered up into an evenly mixed dough ball, a few minutes more.

Cover the bowl with drum-tight plastic wrap and rest overnight on your kitchen counter. In 8 hours or so, a strong, elastic dough will have formed and risen.

Preheat your oven to 425°F (220°C). Turn on your convection fan if you have one. Generously oil a 17- × 11-inch (45 × 29 cm) baking sheet.

Now finish the dough. Gather the dough from the edge and flip it over, deflating it. Transfer to the baking sheet and encourage it into the corners. Dimple the entire surface with your fingers, pushing down until you feel the pan below. Sprinkle with the rosemary and cover evenly with slices of tomato. Sprinkle with salt and pepper.

Rest, uncovered, until the dough rises above the rim of the pan, another hour or so. Bake until golden brown on top and firm, 30 to 40 minutes. Immediately remove the focaccia from the pan. Rest on a rack or cutting board until it's cool enough to handle, then slice.

As the dough rises or bakes, make the tomato butter. Pile the tomatoes into your food processor and pulse briefly into a paste. Add the butter, oregano, parsley and pepper. Continue processing until smooth and vibrant. Spoon into a small festive bowl. Serve with the freshly baked focaccia.

STORAGE TIP

Room Temperature: Cool the focaccia, tightly seal in a zip-top bag and store for up to 4 days. • Tightly seal the butter and store for a few days.

Refrigerator: Tightly seal the butter and refrigerate for up to 14 days.

Freeze: Tightly seal the focaccia and freeze for up to 30 days. Thaw at room temperature for an hour or so. • Tightly seal the butter and freeze for a month or more.

EVERYDAY SALAD WITH MAKE AHEAD DRESSING

An everyday salad is a smart way to keep vegetables front and center in your food world. Keep your fridge and pantry stocked with a few simple essentials so you're poised for salad success any day of the week. One of the secrets to a great salad is to make the dressing in advance. It will gain complexity and nuance as it rests for a day or two. But wait until you're ready to eat before introducing the dressing to the greens. Salad greens begin wilting and losing crispness as soon as they're tossed with acidic dressing. MAKES ONE 2-CUP (500 ML) JAR OF DRESSING, ENOUGH FOR 12 SIDE SALADS, EASILY DOUBLED OR TRIPLED

TODAY FOR TOMORROW   Make the dressing ahead (see Storage Tip). • Prep the vegetables a few days ahead, ready to toss into the salad when the time comes. Refrigerate tightly sealed in a zip-top bag. • Toss together everything but the dressing and store it for a few days, tossing with dressing just before you enjoy it.

FOR THE DRESSING

1 cup (250 mL) of your very best olive oil

½ cup (125 mL) of any vinegar or lemon juice

½ cup (125 mL) of honey, maple syrup or your favorite jam, jelly or marmalade

A heaping spoonful or two of any mustard, even up to ½ cup (125 mL) if you really like mustard

A heaping spoonful or two of your favorite fresh or dried herb, spice, seasoning, condiment or minced garlic or onion

½ teaspoon (2 mL) of salt

Lots of freshly ground pepper

FOR THE SALAD BOWL

Lots of your favorite mixed baby greens, spinach, arugula or any lettuce

Bean sprouts

Shredded carrots

Halved cherry tomatoes

Small broccoli and cauliflower florets

Fresh berries

Thinly sliced apples

Thinly sliced onions

Diced celery

Cooked grains

A can of chickpeas or other beans, drained and well rinsed

CRUNCHY TOPPINGS

Croutons

Nuts

Seeds

Dried fruits

Crushed tortillas

Craft the dressing by measuring all the ingredients into a 2-cup (500 mL) jar and shaking the works to smoothness. The mustard will act as an emulsifier. Keep refrigerated, and shake vigorously just before using.

Fill a large salad bowl or a series of smaller ones with today's greens and additions. Splash on enough dressing to lightly dress the works, just 1 or 2 tablespoons (15 to 30 mL) per serving. Toss everything together and top with the crunch of your choice.

STORAGE TIP

Refrigerate: Tightly seal the dressing and refrigerate for up to 14 days. • Leftover salad starts wilting immediately, but if you don't mind the soft texture, it can be safely enjoyed for days.

MOM'S FAMOUS BEAN SALAD

This salad is one of my earliest taste memories; my mom has been making it my whole life. It's been to every holiday, every picnic, every celebration and every backyard for miles around. I'm not surprised, though, because it is hands-down delicious. Every cook knows that there's often a secret ingredient in their food, one that they can't stir in but is still essential. In this case it's time: the magic transformation that only an overnight rest can bring to this salad. The flavors blend, soften and brighten. MAKES ENOUGH FOR 4 TO 6 SIDE SALADS WITH LEFTOVERS, EASILY DOUBLED OR TRIPLED

TODAY FOR TOMORROW   Prep the vegetables a few days in advance, ready to cook. Refrigerate tightly sealed in a zip-top bag. • Make the dressing and the salad ahead (see Storage Tip).

Whisk together all the dressing ingredients and set aside.

Cut the yellow and green beans into 2-inch (5 cm) lengths. Have ready a large bowl of ice water. Bring a large pot of lightly salted water to a vigorous boil. Add the yellow and green beans and blanch them until their color brightens and texture softens slightly, just 3 or 4 minutes. Drain the beans and immediately plunge them into the ice water to stop the cooking, set their bright color and retain their crispness. Drain again and pat dry.

Toss the blanched beans together with the canned beans, chickpeas, red onion, red pepper and dressing. For best results cover tightly and refrigerate overnight. Serve with a toast to Mom's genius!

STORAGE TIP

Refrigerate: Tightly seal the dressing and refrigerate for up to a week. • Tightly seal the dressed salad in a zip-top bag and refrigerate for up to 6 days.

FOR THE DRESSING

1 cup (250 mL) of sugar

1 cup (250 mL) of cider vinegar

½ cup (125 mL) of vegetable oil

½ teaspoon (2 mL) of salt

Lots of freshly ground pepper

FOR THE SALAD

8 ounces (225 g) of fresh yellow beans, trimmed

8 ounces (225 g) of fresh green beans, trimmed

A 19-ounce (540 mL) can of red kidney beans, drained and well rinsed

A 19-ounce (540 mL) can of chickpeas, drained and well rinsed

1 red onion, thinly sliced

1 red bell pepper, finely diced

ICEBERG WEDGES WITH SRIRACHA BACON AND STEAKHOUSE DRESSING

A cool, crisp wedge of iceberg lettuce is one of the all-stars of the salad world. Here it anchors a classic group of steakhouse flavors that can easily be prepared ahead, ready to go when it's time to impress your table. For maximum crispness and a delightful curly tangled effect, peel the carrots ahead of time and submerge them in cool water. You can leave them in the refrigerator for a few days. MAKES ENOUGH FOR 6 SALADS, DRESSING AND BACON EASILY DOUBLED

TODAY FOR TOMORROW Cook the bacon and make the dressing ahead (see Storage Tip).

FOR THE DRESSING

½ cup (125 mL) of sweet green relish

¼ cup (60 mL) of ketchup

¼ cup (60 mL) of mayonnaise

1 heaping tablespoon (18 mL) of Dijon mustard

1 teaspoon (5 mL) of Worcestershire sauce

¼ teaspoon (1 mL) of Sriracha or your favorite hot sauce

FOR THE BACON

12 thick slices of bacon

Sriracha sauce, as needed

½ cup (125 mL) of brown sugar

FOR THE TOAST

6 slices of hearty country bread

Lots of extra virgin olive oil

FOR THE SALAD

1 head of iceberg lettuce

1 large carrot, peeled, then further peeled into ribbons

Make the dressing by simply stirring all its ingredients together in a jar. Refrigerate until needed.

For the bacon, preheat your oven to 400°F (200°C). Turn on your convection fan if you have one. Line a baking sheet with parchment paper. Neatly align the bacon slices on the paper so their edges closely touch. Squirt a line of Sriracha down the middle of each slice, then evenly sprinkle the works with brown sugar. Bake until crisp, about 20 minutes. Remove from the pan and cool until needed.

Now make the toast. Generously brush both sides of the bread slices with olive oil, then pop into your toaster and toast until golden brown and crisp. Cool. Cut in half before adding to the salad.

To assemble the salad, trim the core out of the lettuce, then cut the head into 6 even wedges. For an alternative presentation, shred the lettuce as finely as you like. Top the lettuce with spoonfuls of dressing, a tangle of carrot ribbons, a few slices of toast and bacon strips.

STORAGE TIP

Refrigerate: Tightly seal the dressing and refrigerate for up to 6 days.
• Tightly seal the bacon and refrigerate for up to 4 days before reheating.

FALL FLAVORS SALAD

This salad is amazing. Its tasty balance of flavors, textures and colors is familiar yet refined. The recipe calls for lots of ingredients, but don't let that stop you—just prepare as much in advance as you can. You'll love being organized and you'll look like a kitchen master when the salad is served.

Toasting spice seeds is a surefire way to remove any staleness and coax out maximum flavor by releasing their flavorful oils. The same thing works for stale pumpkin seeds and all types of often-stale nuts.

MAKES ENOUGH FOR 4 TO 6 SALADS, EASILY DOUBLED OR TRIPLED

TODAY FOR TOMORROW   Toast the seeds and nuts ahead (see Storage Tip). • Make the pickle ahead (see Storage Tip). • Prepare the goat cheese rye crisps a few days in advance and refrigerate until ready to bake.

For the pickle, combine the apple, red onion and dried cranberries in a container with a tight-fitting lid.

Toss the coriander and fennel seeds into a small dry saucepan over medium heat. Gently shake and shiver the works as the seeds begin to toast and pop, 3 or 4 minutes. Add the vinegar, sugar, mustard, hot sauce and salt. Stir together and briefly bring to a furious boil. Pour over the apple mixture, stirring briefly to thoroughly combine. Cover and refrigerate for at least an hour or, for best flavor, overnight.

For the rye crisps, preheat your broiler. Turn on your convection fan if you have one. Spread each bread slice with a spoonful or two of goat cheese. Place on a baking sheet and carefully broil until the cheese bubbles and browns, 3 or 4 minutes. Watch closely—the cheese can quickly progress from tasty golden to burnt bitter. Rest until you're ready to assemble the salad.

To assemble the salad, combine the kale, pickled apples and their pickling liquid in a large salad bowl. Toss everything together until evenly mixed. Either portion into individual bowls or serve family style. Either way, top with the pumpkin seeds and walnuts and nestle in the goat cheese rye crisps.

STORAGE TIP

Room Temperature: Cool toasted seeds and nuts completely, seal tightly in a zip-top bag and store for up to 7 days.

Refrigerate: Tightly seal the pickled apples and refrigerate for up to 6 days.

FOR THE PICKLE

1 green apple, cut into matchsticks or thin slices

1 red onion, thinly sliced

½ cup (125 mL) of dried cranberries

1 tablespoon (15 mL) of coriander seeds

1 tablespoon (15 mL) of fennel seeds

½ cup (125 mL) of cider vinegar

¼ cup (60 mL) of brown sugar

1 tablespoon (15 mL) of Dijon mustard

1 teaspoon (5 mL) of your favorite hot sauce

½ teaspoon (2 mL) of salt

FOR THE GOAT CHEESE RYE CRISPS

6 or 8 slices of rye bread

6 or 8 ounces (170 to 225 g) of goat cheese, softened

FOR THE SALAD

A 5-ounce (142 g) container of baby kale, arugula, spinach or savory salad greens

½ cup (125 mL) of unsalted raw or roasted pumpkin seeds

½ cup (125 mL) of walnut halves

FRENCH LENTIL SALAD WITH DIJON VINAIGRETTE

French cuisine has a way of using the simplest of methods to transform the humblest of ingredients into masterpieces of flavor. Lentils are fervently loved in France, particularly in their home region of the Auvergne, where I too loved this salad at a cobblestone café. And you will love it too. It's delicious, easy to make ahead, inexpensive and nutritious. Especially here at home with our amazing Canadian-grown lentils. MAKES ENOUGH FOR 8 TO 12, EASILY DOUBLED

TODAY FOR TOMORROW All the elements of this salad can be made days in advance: the dressing, the lentil broth, the cooked lentils and the prepped salad vegetables—even the finished salad (see Storage Tip).

FOR THE LENTIL BROTH

2 carrots, thinly sliced

2 onions, thinly sliced

4 bay leaves

8 garlic cloves, smashed

8 sprigs of fresh thyme

8 cups (2 L) of water

FOR THE LENTIL SALAD

2 cups (500 mL) of green lentils

2 large carrots, finely diced

2 celery stalks, finely diced

1 red onion, minced

1 cup (250 mL) of finely chopped fresh parsley

FOR THE VINAIGRETTE

½ cup (125 mL) of extra virgin olive oil

¼ cup (60 mL) of your best red wine, white wine or champagne vinegar

¼ cup (60 mL) of Dijon mustard

2 tablespoons (30 mL) of dried tarragon

2 tablespoons (30 mL) of honey

½ teaspoon (2 mL) of salt

Lots of freshly ground pepper

Begin by crafting a flavorful cooking broth for the lentils. Fill a pot with the carrots, onion, bay leaves, garlic, thyme and water. Bring to a furious boil, then reduce the heat to a simmer, cover and simmer for about 30 minutes. Turn off the heat and rest for another 30 minutes or so for maximum flavor extraction. Strain the broth through a fine-mesh strainer into a large saucepan and bring back to a simmer. Discard the solids.

For the lentil salad, toss the lentils into the simmering broth and cook them, uncovered, until they're just barely tender, even a tad al dente, about 20 minutes. Add the carrots, celery and onion and continue simmering just long enough for the flavors to brighten and textures to soften, 2 minutes more. Drain, then let rest for a few moments of drying. Transfer to a festive salad bowl.

While the broth or lentils are simmering, even days before, craft the vinaigrette. Whisk together all the ingredients until a smooth dressing forms.

Pour the dressing over the lentils and toss the works until thoroughly combined. Rest as long as you can, even overnight. For a burst of fresh flavor, toss in the parsley just before you serve.

STORAGE TIP

Refrigerate: Tightly seal the lentil broth and refrigerate for up to 6 days. • Tightly seal the cooked lentils and refrigerate for up to 6 days. • Tightly seal the prepared vegetables in a zip-top bag and refrigerate for up to 3 days. • Tightly seal the dressing and refrigerate for up to 6 days. • Tightly seal the dressed salad and refrigerate for up to 6 days.

SMOKED SALMON POTATO SALAD WITH ANCHOVY DRESSING

When you live in potato country, you learn a few things about Prince Edward Island's treasured tuber. You learn that everybody says their mom's potato salad is the best. You learn not to argue. You learn not to reveal that there are anchovies in the dressing until the plates are licked clean and the pencils are out for the recipe.

This salad tastes noticeably better when made ahead. The savory umami flavors of the anchovies need a chance to fully emerge and balance the sour lemon and other dressing tastes. Then the potatoes need time to absorb that dressing so their luxurious texture can also emerge. I prefer to use russets or Yukon Gold potatoes in this salad. MAKES 6 TO 8 MAIN-COURSE SALADS OR SIDES, EASILY DOUBLED

TODAY FOR TOMORROW Make the dressing and the salad ahead (see Storage Tip).

3 pounds (1.3 kg) of your favorite potatoes, unpeeled, scrubbed and cut into bite-size cubes

THE DRESSING

A 2-ounce (56 g) can of anchovies and every last drop of oil in it

1 cup (250 mL) of mayonnaise

1 heaping tablespoon (18 mL) of yellow mustard

1 overflowing teaspoon (6 mL) of Worcestershire sauce

4 green onions, thinly sliced

2 celery stalks, finely diced

The zest and juice of 2 lemons

½ cup (125 mL) of sweet green relish

1 teaspoon (5 mL) of salt

Lots of freshly ground pepper

12 ounces (340 g) of your favorite smoked salmon, sliced

Bring a large pot of salted water to a furious boil. Slip in the potatoes and cook until a fork pierces them easily, 10 to 15 minutes. Drain the potatoes and spread them on a lightly oiled or parchment-lined baking sheet to cool in your fridge or on the counter.

Make the dressing while the potatoes cool. In a blender, purée the anchovies and their oil, mayonnaise, mustard and Worcestershire sauce until silky smooth. (You can add a splash of water to get things going or use your food processor instead.) Pour into a large bowl and add the green onions, celery, lemon zest and juice, relish, and salt and pepper. Stir together thoroughly. When the potatoes are cool, gently toss them in the dressing until evenly coated. There may seem to be a lot of dressing, but as the salad rests the potatoes will absorb every drop.

To serve, drape a few slices of rich smoked salmon over a mound of the salad.

STORAGE TIP

Refrigerate: Tightly seal the dressing and refrigerate for up to 2 days. • Tightly seal the salad and refrigerate for up to 4 days.

SOUPS, STEWS AND SLOW COOKING

SOUPS, STEWS AND SLOW COOKING RECIPES

COCONUT SHRIMP SOUP WITH THAI FLAVORS AND RICE NOODLES

Few cooks fill a bowl with such brightly balanced flavors as well as the Thais do. Among the many secrets of Thai cooking is this dish's finishing flourish of warm spicy broth poured over a crisp, fresh salad. A great way to feed a crowd or gear up for the lunchboxes in your life. MAKES 6 TO 8 BOWLS, EASILY DOUBLED

TODAY FOR TOMORROW Pick a weekend. Prepare and package the broth, vegetables and noodles into a daily pair of mason jars, one for the broth, the other for your daily dose of noodles plus the salad garnish on top. Heat the broth (maybe in a microwave), then pour into the noodle jar, soaking the noodles below the salad. Let stand 5 minutes, then stir with chopsticks. • Fully cook this dish now and reheat anytime during the next several days, or freeze (see Storage Tip).

FOR THE SHRIMP BROTH AND NOODLES

A splash of vegetable oil

2 onions, finely chopped

1 red bell pepper, cut into short, thin strips

2 carrots, grated

2 garlic cloves, minced

1 tablespoon (15 mL) of your favorite Thai green, yellow or red curry paste

A 14-ounce (400 mL) can of coconut milk with cream

2 cups (500 mL) of Homemade Chicken Broth (page 201), a low-sodium store-bought substitute or water

2 tablespoons (30 mL) of fish sauce

The zest and juice of 1 lime

4 lime leaves

1 pound (450 g) of shell-on shrimp, deveined

7 ounces (200 g) or so of rice stick noodles

1 teaspoon (5 mL) of toasted sesame oil

FOR EACH BOWL'S SALAD GARNISH

A handful of bean sprouts, rinsed

6 or 8 snow peas, thinly sliced

A handful of chopped peanuts

A lime wedge

A handful of tender fresh cilantro sprigs

Start with the shrimp broth. Splash a little vegetable oil into a large soup pot over medium-high heat. Toss in the onions, red pepper, carrots and garlic. Stir-fry briefly until their flavors brighten, 2 or 3 minutes. Stir in the curry paste and toast for a few moments, awakening and blooming its flavors.

Pour in the coconut milk, chicken broth, fish sauce, lime zest and juice, and lime leaves. Bring to a furious boil, then reduce the heat to a simmer and stir in the shrimp. Simmer until the shrimp is cooked through, about 5 minutes. Remove from the heat.

When you're ready to assemble the dish, cook the noodles in lots of boiling water until tender yet firm, about 5 minutes. Drain and toss with the sesame oil to keep them from sticking. Add a handful to each serving bowl and top with bean sprouts, snow peas and ladlefuls of shrimp broth. Sprinkle with peanuts, tuck in a lime wedge and perch cilantro on top.

STORAGE TIP

Refrigerate: Tightly seal the broth and garnishes separately and refrigerate within 30 minutes of cooking. Store for up to 4 days before reheating.

Freeze: Portion the finished broth, tightly seal and freeze for up to 30 days. Thaw in the refrigerator for 1 or 2 days before reheating with fresh garnishes. Tightly seal leftovers and store in the refrigerator for just a few days.

VEGETARIAN MINESTRONE WITH NOT-SO-VEGETARIAN ANCHOVY HUMMUS SWIRL

A good minestrone is a quick way to fill a pot with lots to eat. A great minestrone is so packed full of rich vegetable flavor that you can leave out the meat and no one will miss it. This one definitely falls into the great category, with or without the swirl. Minestrone is always dramatically better the next day, after the flavors have come together and evolved. MAKES ENOUGH FOR 12 TO 16 BOWLS, EASILY DOUBLED IN A VERY LARGE POT

TODAY FOR TOMORROW Prep the vegetables a few days in advance, ready to cook when the time comes. Refrigerate tightly sealed in a zip-top bag. • Make the soup and the hummus ahead (see Storage Tip). • Fully cook this dish now and reheat anytime during the next several days (see Storage Tip).

FOR THE MINESTRONE

2 tablespoons (30 mL) of olive oil

2 red bell peppers, diced

2 onions, finely chopped

2 carrots, diced

2 celery stalks, diced

4 garlic cloves, minced

4 cups (1 L) of vegetable broth, Homemade Chicken Broth (page 201), a low-sodium store-bought substitute or water

4 cups (1 L) of tomato juice

A 28-ounce (796 mL) can of diced tomatoes

A 19-ounce (540 mL) can of white kidney beans, drained and well rinsed

1 tablespoon (15 mL) of dried oregano

2 teaspoons (10 mL) of salt

Lots of freshly ground pepper

1 cup (250 mL) of orzo

1 cup (250 mL) of fresh or frozen green beans, cut into 1-inch (2.5 cm) lengths

1 bunch of kale, central ribs removed, leaves torn into bite-size pieces

2 zucchini, diced

FOR THE ANCHOVY HUMMUS

A 19-ounce (540 mL) can of chickpeas, drained and well rinsed

1 tablespoon (15 mL) of your favorite hot sauce

½ cup (125 mL) of extra virgin olive oil

A 2-ounce (56 g) can of anchovies and every last drop of oil in it

The zest and juice of 1 lemon

For the minestrone, splash the olive oil into a large soup pot over medium-high heat. Toss in the red pepper, onions, carrots, celery and garlic and cook, stirring, until the vegetable flavors awaken and brighten, 4 or 5 minutes.

Add the broth, tomato juice, canned tomatoes with their juice, kidney beans, oregano, salt and pepper. Briefly bring to a furious boil, then reduce the heat and slowly simmer for 20 minutes or so. Stir in the orzo, green beans, kale and zucchini. Simmer until the orzo is tender, about 10 minutes.

Meanwhile, add all the hummus ingredients to your food processor and process until smooth.

Swirl big dollops of hummus into steaming bowls of minestrone.

STORAGE TIP

Refrigerate: Tightly seal the soup and refrigerate within 30 minutes of cooking. Store for up to 6 days before reheating. • Tightly seal the hummus and refrigerate for up to 7 days.

Freeze: Portion the soup, tightly seal and freeze for up to 30 days. Reheat straight from the freezer or thaw in the refrigerator for 1 or 2 days before reheating. Tightly seal leftovers and store in the refrigerator for just a few days.

BAKED REUBEN CHOWDER

If you are a fan of the sandwich, try this twist. The Reuben's classic flavors are, not surprisingly, just as delicious together in a soup. If you can't figure out which version you prefer, just make them both and enjoy together! Soup always goes with a sandwich. This showstopper can be fully prepared in advance.
MAKES ENOUGH FOR 8 TO 12 BOWLS, EASILY DOUBLED

TODAY FOR TOMORROW   Grate the cheese and slice the bread a few days in advance. Seal tightly in separate zip-top bags.
• Make the chowder ahead and reheat anytime during the next several days (see Storage Tip).

FOR THE REUBEN CHOWDER

¼ cup (60 mL) of butter

2 large onions, chopped

4 garlic cloves, minced

4 or 5 tablespoons (60 to 75 mL) of all-purpose flour

4 cups (1 L) of Homemade Chicken Broth (page 201) or a low-sodium store-bought substitute

1½ pounds (675 g) of any potatoes, peeled and diced

4 cups (1 L) of water or more real chicken broth

1 cup (250 mL) of whipping cream

1 pound (450 g) of your favorite pastrami, sliced and cut into bite-size pieces

2 cups (500 mL) of drained sauerkraut

2 or 3 bay leaves

1 teaspoon (5 mL) of salt

4 or 5 green onions, thinly sliced

TO FINISH EACH BOWL

8 to 12 slices of rye bread, toasted

16 to 24 ounces (450 to 675 g) of sliced Swiss or grated Gruyère cheese (about 2 ounces/55 g per serving)

Toss the butter into a large soup pot over medium heat. Swirl it gently as it melts, then toss in the onions and garlic and sauté, stirring with a wooden spoon, until their flavors brighten, 2 or 3 minutes. Sprinkle the flour over the vegetables and stir to form a thick paste. Vigorously whisk in 4 cups (1 L) of broth, then add the potatoes. Briefly bring to a furious boil, then reduce the heat to a slow, steady simmer. Continue simmering until the potatoes are tender, 10 minutes or so. Add the water, cream, pastrami, sauerkraut, bay leaves and salt. Briefly bring the works to a furious boil. Reduce the heat and simmer for a few moments. Stir in the green onions and the soup is done.

Preheat your broiler and position a rack near the top. Neatly arrange ovenproof bowls on a baking sheet. Ladle in enough soup to nearly fill each bowl. Top with a neatly trimmed layer of rye toast mounded with a thick layer of grated cheese. Carefully broil until the cheese is melted, bubbling and thoroughly golden brown, 5 minutes or so. Serve immediately.

STORAGE TIP

Refrigerate: Tightly seal the chowder—with or without the green onions—and refrigerate within 30 minutes of cooking. Store for up to 6 days before reheating.

Freeze: Portion the chowder, tightly seal and freeze for up to 30 days. Reheat straight from the freezer or thaw in the refrigerator for 1 or 2 days before reheating. Tightly seal leftovers and store in the refrigerator for just a few days.

ORANGE FENNEL MUSSEL BROTH WITH SAFFRON, VANILLA AND BASIL

In all the world of cooking, few things are easier to cook than mussels and few flavor combos tastier than fennel, saffron, basil and—surprisingly—vanilla. After you add the mussels, taste the soup, then stir in the vanilla and basil and taste again. You'll be amazed at the transformation, the smoothness the vanilla brings without asserting itself. What a delicious way to fill a soup bowl! Saffron is not only the world's most expensive spice, it's also perhaps the most intensely fragrant. But it can be a bit shy. If you make this soup in advance, you'll give the saffron extra time to emerge. MAKES ENOUGH FOR 4 BOWLS, EASILY DOUBLED

TODAY FOR TOMORROW   Make the broth ahead (see Storage Tip). • Fully cook this soup now and reheat anytime during the next several days (see Storage Tip). • Steam the mussels now, to be added to the broth later: In a big pot, combine mussels and ½ cup (125 mL) or more white wine. Steam until mussels open, then wait until they are cool enough to handle. Discard any mussels that don't open. Remove mussels from shells and refrigerate or freeze in their own broth.

Start with the broth. Trim and reserve the fennel fronds. Neatly dice the stems and thinly slice the bulb crosswise or lengthwise. Toss the butter into a large soup pot over medium heat, swirling gently as it melts. Add the fennel stalks, fennel seeds and saffron. Stir as their licorice-like flavors brighten, 2 or 3 minutes. Add the garlic and sliced fennel bulb and stir for a few minutes more. Pour in the wine, cream, orange zest and juice, and salt. Briefly bring to a furious boil, then back off to a slow, steady simmer.

To finish the soup, add the mussels to the broth and simmer until they steam open, releasing their delicious broth into the soup. Discard any mussels that don't open. For a bit of finesse, shuck the mussels back into the soup and discard the shells. Stir in the vanilla and basil. Mince the reserved fennel fronds and sprinkle over every bowl with a splash of Pernod.

STORAGE TIP

Refrigerate: Tightly seal the broth and refrigerate within 30 minutes of cooking. Store for up to 6 days before reheating. • Tightly seal the finished soup and refrigerate within 30 minutes of cooking. Store for up to 4 days before reheating.

Freeze: Portion the broth or finished soup, tightly seal and freeze for up to 30 days. Reheat straight from the freezer or thaw in the refrigerator for 1 or 2 days before reheating. Tightly seal leftovers and store in the refrigerator for just a few days.

THE BROTH

1 large fennel bulb

2 tablespoons (30 mL) of butter

1 heaping tablespoon (18 mL) of fennel seeds

As many saffron threads as you can cram in a teaspoon

4 garlic cloves, minced

1 overflowing cup (275 mL) of white wine

1 cup (250 mL) of whipping cream

The zest of 2 or 3 oranges

1 cup (250 mL) of orange juice

½ teaspoon (2 mL) of salt

TO FINISH THE SOUP

5 pounds (2.25 kg) or so of fresh Prince Edward Island mussels, rinsed and drained

1 teaspoon (5 mL) of pure vanilla extract

1 or 2 large bunches of fresh basil, tender stems and all, thinly sliced

A few splashes of Pernod or other anise-flavored liqueur

BACON CHEDDAR CORN CHOWDER

Even on Prince Edward Island we'll admit that you can make chowder without seafood. But the only acceptable alternative is corn, and it's even better with smoked cheddar and bacon! For even more flavor, do what the pros do: Shave the kernels off 4 fresh corn cobs, break the cobs into 2 or 3 pieces each and simmer, covered, within the chicken broth, cream and milk. Add to the soup along with the potatoes. The cobs are packed with just as much fresh corn flavor as their kernels. MAKES ENOUGH FOR 6 TO 8 HEARTY BOWLS, EASILY DOUBLED

TODAY FOR TOMORROW Prep the bacon and vegetables a few days in advance. Refrigerate in separate zip-top bags.
• Fully cook this dish now and reheat anytime during the next several days (see Storage Tip).

FOR THE CHOWDER BASE

8 thick slices of bacon, cut into thin strips

2 or 3 large onions, finely chopped

2 celery stalks, finely diced

4 garlic cloves, minced

¼ teaspoon (1 mL) of salt

Lots of freshly ground pepper

1½ pounds (675 g) of potatoes, unpeeled, scrubbed and diced

2 cups (500 mL) of Homemade Chicken Broth (page 201), a low-sodium store-bought substitute or water

4 cups (1 L) of frozen corn (or kernels from 4 to 6 fresh cobs)

A 12-ounce (350 mL) can of evaporated milk

1 cup (250 mL) of milk or cream

Leaves from 6 or 8 sprigs of fresh thyme, minced

TO FINISH AND GARNISH THE CHOWDER

1 bunch of fresh parsley, chopped

4 green onions, thinly sliced

8 ounces (225 g) of smoked or other cheddar cheese, grated

Toss the bacon and a big splash of water into a large soup pot over medium-high heat. Cook until the bacon is fully browned and evenly crispy, 10 minutes or so. Add the onions, celery, garlic, salt and pepper and lightly sauté, releasing and brightening their flavors.

Add the potatoes and chicken broth. Briefly bring to a furious boil, then reduce the heat to a slow, steady simmer and cook until the potatoes are tender, about 15 minutes. Stir in the corn, evaporated milk, milk and thyme. Return to a simmer.

To finish the soup, stir in most of the parsley and green onions and half of the cheese. Ladle the chowder into bowls and sprinkle with the remaining cheese, green onions and parsley.

STORAGE TIP

Refrigerate: Tightly seal the finished chowder and refrigerate within 30 minutes of cooking. Store for up to 6 days before reheating.

Freeze: Portion the finished chowder, tightly seal and freeze for up to 30 days. Reheat straight from the freezer or thaw in the refrigerator for 1 or 2 days before reheating. Tightly seal leftovers and store in the refrigerator for just a few days.

SWEET POTATO SOUP AND PUMPKIN SEED PESTO

Soups are super simple to make ahead, especially when you know you're packing them with this much nutritional intensity and flavor. Sweet potatoes are crammed with gloriously healthy flavor, bright color and smooth texture. They really are perfect for soup. Of course, this brightly flavored pesto doesn't hurt either! MAKES ENOUGH FOR 6 BOWLS, EASILY DOUBLED

TODAY FOR TOMORROW Make the soup and the pesto ahead (see Storage Tip). • Fully cook this soup now and reheat anytime during the next several days (see Storage Tip).

Toss the butter into a large pot over medium-high heat, swirling it gently as it melts. Add the onions, garlic, ginger, cinnamon, nutmeg, salt and pepper; sauté just long enough to brighten the flavors, 2 or 3 minutes. Pour in the chicken broth and cream. Stir in the sweet potatoes. Briefly bring the works to a furious boil, then reduce the heat to a slow, steady simmer, cover and simmer until the sweet potatoes are tender, about 15 minutes.

Working in batches if you need to, carefully purée the hot soup as smoothly as you can using an immersion blender, a blender or food processor. (A good old-fashioned mashing ain't bad either!)

Make the pesto while the soup simmers. Dump everything into your food processor. Purée until smooth, scraping the sides down once or twice.

Ladle the soup into festive bowls and dollop a spoonful or two of the pesto into each bowl.

STORAGE TIP

Refrigerate: Tightly seal the soup and refrigerate within 30 minutes of cooking. Store for up to 6 days before reheating. • Tightly seal the pesto and refrigerate for up to a week.

Freeze: Portion the soup, tightly seal and freeze for up to 30 days. Reheat straight from the freezer or thaw in the refrigerator for 1 or 2 days before reheating. Tightly seal leftovers and store in the refrigerator for just a few days. • Tightly seal the pesto and freeze up to a month.

FOR THE SOUP

¼ cup (60 mL) of butter

2 onions, finely chopped

4 or 5 garlic cloves, minced

1 teaspoon (5 mL) of grated frozen ginger

1 teaspoon (5 mL) of cinnamon

½ teaspoon (2 mL) of nutmeg

1 teaspoon (5 mL) of salt

Lots of freshly ground pepper

4 cups (1 L) of Homemade Chicken Broth (page 201), a low-sodium store-bought substitute or water

1 cup (250 mL) of whipping cream

4 pounds (1.8 kg) of sweet potatoes, peeled and grated or finely chopped

FOR THE PESTO

1 cup (250 mL) of unsalted roasted pumpkin seeds

½ cup (125 mL) of finely grated Parmigiano-Reggiano cheese

¼ cup (60 mL) of extra virgin olive oil

2 green onions, chopped

8 fresh sage leaves

SLOW SPLIT PEA SOUP

Split pea soup is for sharing—and saving for even more sharing. Its humble ingredients probably have something to do with why it's so richly deserving of its status as a true soup icon. Like many slow-cooker dishes, you can fill your crock with the ingredients, then refrigerate overnight or even for a few days before dropping it into the slow-cooker base and cooking it. If you don't have spilt peas, lentils are always a great substitute. MAKES 6 OR 8 BOWLS, EASILY DOUBLED

TODAY FOR TOMORROW Prep the vegetables a few days in advance, ready to toss into the soup. Refrigerate tightly sealed in a zip-top bag. • Make this soup ahead (see Storage Tip). • Fully cook this dish now and reheat anytime during the next several days (see Storage Tip).

2 cups (500 mL) of green split
   peas, rinsed and picked over

A smoked ham hock
   (about 1½ pounds/675 g)

2 large onions, finely chopped

2 carrots, diced

2 celery stalks, diced

4 or 5 garlic cloves, thinly sliced

2 bay leaves

Lots of freshly ground pepper

8 cups (2 L) of water

Leaves from 3 or 4 fresh
   thyme sprigs, minced

1 cup (250 mL) of frozen peas

1 tablespoon (15 mL) of
   any vinegar

Pour the split peas into your slow cooker. Nestle the ham hock into the legumes. Pile in the onions, carrots, celery and garlic. Nestle in the bay leaves and season with pepper—no salt necessary, there's plenty in the ham hock. Pour in the water and set your slow cooker to low and walk away for about 10 hours.

Fish out the ham hock and discard the skin, bones and any cartilage. Shred the meat and return it to the soup. Discard the bay leaves. To balance and brighten the flavors, stir in the thyme, frozen peas and vinegar.

STORAGE TIP

Refrigerate: Tightly seal the soup and refrigerate within 30 minutes of cooking. Store for up to 6 days before reheating.

Freeze: Portion, tightly seal and freeze for up to 30 days. Reheat straight from the freezer or thaw in the refrigerator for 1 or 2 days before reheating. Tightly seal leftovers and store in the refrigerator for just a few days.

BEEFY BARLEY KALE STEW

The rich flavors of browned beef only get better when they're stewed with tender barley and finished with hearty kale. This stew is comfort food at its best—rich and satisfying, hearty and healthy, and filled with fresh green flavor. Add just about any other green vegetable you can think of: broccoli, asparagus, peas, edamame, savory greens, Brussels sprouts. MAKES 8 BOWLS, EASILY DOUBLED IN A LARGER POT

TODAY FOR TOMORROW Prep the vegetables a few days in advance. Refrigerate tightly sealed in a zip-top bag.
• Fully cook the stew now and reheat anytime during the next several days (see Storage Tip).

Heat your largest thick-bottomed pot over medium-high heat while you gently dry the beef on a few paper towels. Splash a pool of oil into the pot, swirling to cover the bottom with a thin film. Without crowding the pan, carefully add a single sizzling layer of beef. This is your only shot at adding the rich, deep flavors that can only come from respectfully browned meat. Listen to the heat. Sizzle is the sound of flavor. Too loud, though, and a sizzling pan becomes a smoking-burning pan. When the beef is deeply browned all over, transfer it to a plate. Repeat with the rest of the beef, 10 to 15 minutes in total. Pour off any excess oil, leaving behind any browned bits of goodness.

Add the onions, carrots, celery, garlic, tomato paste, water, wine, bay leaf, salt and pepper. Return the beef and any juices to the pot. Stirring occasionally, briefly bring the works to a furious boil, then reduce the heat to a slow, steady simmer. Cover tightly and gently simmer for an hour or so, stirring now and then, patiently tenderizing the meat, releasing its richness and building deep beefy flavor.

Stir in the barley and cook for another hour or until the beef is meltingly tender and the barley deliciously chewy.

When it's time to eat, discard the bay leaf and return to a simmer. Stir in the thyme and kale, cover, turn off the heat and rest just long enough to wilt the greens, a minute or two. Serve with lots of sharp horseradish.

STORAGE TIP

Refrigerate: Tightly seal the stew and refrigerate within 30 minutes of cooking. Store for up to 6 days before reheating.

Freeze: Portion, tightly seal and freeze for up to 30 days. Reheat straight from the freezer or thaw in the refrigerator for 1 or 2 days before reheating. Tightly seal leftovers and store in the refrigerator for just a few days.

2 pounds (900 g) of stewing beef, cut into roughly 1-inch (2.5 cm) cubes

A few generous splashes of vegetable oil

2 onions, chopped

2 carrots, chopped

2 celery stalks, chopped

4 garlic cloves, thinly sliced

A 5½-ounce (156 mL) can of tomato paste

8 cups (2 L) of water

2 cups (500 mL) of red wine

1 bay leaf

2 teaspoons (10 mL) of salt

Lots of freshly ground pepper

1 cup (250 mL) of barley

Leaves from 4 or 5 sprigs of fresh thyme

1 bunch of kale, tough center ribs removed, leaves torn or cut into small bite-size pieces

Prepared horseradish

BEEF STROGANOFF WITH PARSLEY NOODLES

This is one of the world's great beef stews. You just can't go wrong with a patiently simmered, richly finished beefy bowl of flavor ladled over addictively slurpy noodles. That's a winning formula anywhere on the globe—especially in your kitchen. You can use any beef stewing meat, but try boneless blade roast for big, beefy flavor. MAKES 4 TO 6 BOWLS, EASILY DOUBLED

TODAY FOR TOMORROW Prep the vegetables a few days in advance. Refrigerate tightly sealed in a zip-top bag. • Make the stroganoff sauce, without the sour cream, ahead (see Storage Tip). • Fully cook the stroganoff and noodles now and reheat anytime during the next several days (see Storage Tip).

Preheat your oven to 325°F (160°C). Turn on your convection fan if you have one.

Heat your largest thick-bottomed pot or Dutch oven over medium-high heat while you gently dry the beef on a few paper towels. Splash a pool of oil into the pot, swirling to cover the bottom with a thin film. Without crowding the pan, carefully add a single sizzling layer of beef. When the meat is deeply browned, transfer it to a plate. Repeat with the rest of the beef, 10 to 15 minutes in total.

Add the mushrooms and onions and continue cooking until they're lightly browned and fragrant. Stir in the garlic near the end so it doesn't scorch. Return the beef and any juices to the pot and add the beef broth, red wine, tomato paste, Worcestershire sauce, mustard, salt and pepper. Stirring frequently, briefly bring the works to a furious boil, then reduce the heat to a slow, steady simmer. Cover tightly and place in the oven. Braise for an hour or so, patiently tenderizing the meat and building deep beefy flavor.

Remove the lid and continue braising for 15 minutes more. These last few minutes nudge the meat from good to meltingly tender, and the sauce from blander to rich and unctuous.

Meanwhile, bring a large pot of salted water to a furious boil. Toss in the noodles and cook until al dente, no more than 8 to 10 minutes. At the same time, toss the butter into a small saucepan over medium-high heat and swirl until melted and fragrant. Add the garlic and continue to swirl just long enough to awaken its pungent flavor, 1 or 2 minutes. Drain the noodles well, return to the pot, and quickly stir in the garlic butter and parsley.

Stir the sour cream into the stroganoff. Generously ladle the sauce over the noodles.

FOR THE STROGANOFF

A few splashes of vegetable oil

2 pounds (900 g) of beef stewing meat, cut into bite-size cubes

1 pound (450 g) of button mushrooms, quartered

4 onions, chopped

4 garlic cloves, minced

2 cups (500 mL) of real beef broth, a low-sodium store-bought substitute or water

1 cup (250 mL) of red wine

A 5½-ounce (156 mL) can of tomato paste

1 tablespoon (15 mL) of Worcestershire sauce

1 tablespoon (15 mL) of Dijon mustard

1 teaspoon (5 mL) of salt

Lots of freshly ground pepper

½ cup (125 mL) of sour cream

FOR THE NOODLES

1 pound (450 g) of egg noodles

2 tablespoons (30 mL) of butter

2 garlic cloves, finely minced

1 bunch of fresh parsley, finely minced

STORAGE TIP

Refrigerate: Tightly seal the sauce—without the sour cream—and refrigerate within 30 minutes of cooking. Store for up to 6 days before reheating and finishing with the sour cream.

Freeze: Portion, tightly seal and freeze for up to 30 days. Reheat straight from the freezer or thaw in the refrigerator for 1 or 2 days before reheating. Tightly seal leftovers and store in the refrigerator for just a few days.

BACON CHIPOTLE CHILI

Bacon in chili? Really? Of course! Chipotle chilies too. And all the usual suspects help you fill your bowl with big flavor. You're making a lot because you can and must when chili is this deliciously spicy. MAKES ENOUGH FOR 12 TO 15, EASILY DOUBLED

TODAY FOR TOMORROW Fully cook the chili now and reheat anytime during the next several days (see Storage Tip).

8 thick slices of bacon, cut into thin strips

2 onions, chopped

4 or 5 garlic cloves, minced

2 tablespoons (30 mL) of chili powder

1 tablespoon (15 mL) of paprika

1 tablespoon (15 mL) of ground cumin

1 tablespoon (15 mL) of dried oregano

2 pounds (900 g) of medium ground beef

2 cans (28 ounces/796 mL each) of diced tomatoes

2 cans (19 ounces/540 mL each) of black or red kidney beans, drained and well rinsed

2 chipotle chilies in adobo sauce, minced

2 red bell peppers, chopped

2 teaspoons (10 mL) of salt

Toss the bacon and a big splash of water into a large stew pot over medium-high heat. Cook until the bacon is fully browned and evenly crispy, 10 minutes or so. Stir in the onions, garlic, chili powder, paprika, cumin and oregano; cook until fragrant, a few minutes.

Add the ground beef and 1 can of tomatoes with their juice for moisture. Stir vigorously until the meat is completely broken up and evenly mixed together. Add the remaining tomatoes, the beans, chipotle chilies, red peppers and salt. Briefly bring to a furious boil, then reduce the heat to a slow, steady simmer. Cover and cook until the meat is tender, an hour or so.

STORAGE TIP

Refrigerate: Tightly seal the chili and refrigerate within 30 minutes of cooking. Store for up to 6 days before reheating.

Freeze: Portion, tightly seal and freeze for up to 30 days. Reheat straight from the freezer or thaw in the refrigerator for 1 or 2 days before reheating. Tightly seal leftovers and store in the refrigerator for just a few days.

CROCKPOT CHICKEN, BARLEY AND LEEKS

This may sound like just another chicken dish, but it's really a leek dish masquerading as a chicken dish. There's some tender barley tossed in for chewy contrast, but the leeks really steal the show as they slowly melt into the dish as they cook.

Of all the make ahead things you can do to save time in making meals, none is as useful as making a batch of good old-fashioned homemade chicken broth. MAKES ENOUGH FOR 6 TO 8, EASILY DOUBLED

TODAY FOR TOMORROW Cook the chicken thoroughly a few days in advance. Refrigerate with the wine-deglazed juices from the browning pan. • Fully cook the stew now and reheat anytime during the next several days (see Storage Tip).

8 boneless, skinless chicken thighs or 4 full legs

1 teaspoon (5 mL) of salt

Lots of freshly ground pepper

1 cup (250 mL) of all-purpose flour

A few splashes of vegetable oil

½ cup (125 mL) of white wine

1 cup (250 mL) of barley

4 large leeks (white and pale green parts only), trimmed and halved lengthwise

4 to 6 cups (1 to 1.5 L) of Homemade Chicken Broth (page 201), a low-sodium store-bought substitute or water

2 or 3 bay leaves

4 garlic cloves, thinly sliced

Leaves from 10 or 12 sprigs of fresh thyme, chopped

Generously season the chicken and thoroughly dredge it in the flour, shaking off the excess. Splash a few spoonfuls of oil into a large skillet over medium-high heat. Add the chicken and cook until fully browned and thoroughly crispy. Transfer to a plate as cooked.

Pour the wine into the sizzling pan and stir loose every single bit of browned flavor. Pour into your slow cooker. Top with an even layer of barley. Neatly nestle in the leeks, and cover those with the browned chicken. Add the chicken broth, bay leaves and garlic. Cook on any setting until the chicken is tender and the barley is cooked, 6 to 8 hours or more, depending on your slow cooker.

At the appointed hour, fish out the bay leaves and stir in the fresh thyme.

STORAGE TIP

Refrigerate: Tightly seal the browned chicken and refrigerate within 30 minutes of cooking. Store for up to 3 days before continuing. • Tightly seal the finished stew and refrigerate within 30 minutes of cooking. Store for up to 6 days.

Freeze: Portion the finished stew, tightly seal and freeze for up to 30 days. Reheat straight from the freezer or thaw in the refrigerator for 1 or 2 days before reheating. Tightly seal leftovers and store in the refrigerator for just a few days.

BARBECUE BAKED BEANS

This is one of my all-time favorite ways to bake a batch of beans. It's particularly popular at potlucks and always the first pot to empty. It's so easy to cook your own beans and avoid the high-sodium and mushy canned ones.

If you forget to soak your beans the night before, you can jump-start them by bringing them to a furious boil in an equal amount of water before turning off the heat and resting them, covered, for 1 hour of rapid rehydration. Drain well, then carry on with your recipe. MAKES 8 TO 10 MAINS OR 12 TO 16 SIDES, EASILY DOUBLED IN A LARGE SLOW COOKER

TODAY FOR TOMORROW Soak the beans ahead of time. • Bake the beans now and reheat anytime during the next several days (see Storage Tip).

6 cups (1.5 L) of white beans, soaked overnight in lots of water

8 slices of bacon, cut into bite-size pieces

4 large onions, chopped

8 garlic cloves, minced

6 cups (1.5 L) of water

2 cups (500 mL) of premium barbecue sauce

1 cup (250 mL) of yellow mustard

1 tablespoon (15 mL) of ground cumin

1 tablespoon (15 mL) of paprika

1 tablespoon (15 mL) of your favorite hot sauce

Drain and rinse the beans. Toss the bacon and a big splash of water into a large skillet over medium-high heat. Cook until the bacon is fully browned and evenly crispy, 10 minutes or so. Stir in the onions and garlic; lightly brown them. Transfer to your slow cooker. Add the beans, pour in the water and stir in the barbecue sauce, mustard, cumin, paprika and hot sauce. Set the slow cooker to its lowest setting and bake the beans for 8 to 10 hours.

STORAGE TIP

Refrigerate: Tightly seal the baked beans and refrigerate within 30 minutes of cooking. Store for up to 6 days before reheating.

Freeze: Portion, tightly seal and freeze for up to 30 days. Reheat straight from the freezer or thaw in the refrigerator for 1 or 2 days before reheating. Tightly seal leftovers and store in the refrigerator for just a few days.

DINNER
DISHES

DINNER DISHES RECIPES

REALLY BIG LASAGNA

Old-school lasagna is a bit of a project, so if you're going to gear up you might as well go large and make a lot. Especially when your recipe is delicious. Think infinite tasty leftovers and get to work! If you can't polish off this 15-pound monstrosity of meat sauce and pasta mayhem, cool the works, then cut into easily refrigerated or frozen portions. Instead of one large pan you can make two smaller 13- × 9-inch (3.5 L) pans and freeze one. You can also assemble the works in small foil containers. MAKES ENOUGH FOR 24 SLICES, YOU'LL NEED ANOTHER GIANT PAN TO DOUBLE THE WORKS

TODAY FOR TOMORROW Cook the meat sauce and the cheese sauce a few days in advance, ready for assembly (see Storage Tip). • Fully cook this dish now and reheat anytime during the next several days (see Storage Tip).

FOR THE MEAT SAUCE

A generous splash of vegetable oil

4 onions, chopped

Cloves from 1 head of garlic, thinly sliced

2 pounds (900 g) of medium ground beef

The meat from 8 spicy Italian sausages

2 cans (28 ounces/796 mL each) of crushed tomatoes

2 cups (500 mL) of Homemade Chicken Broth (page 201), beef broth or a low-sodium store-bought substitute

¼ cup (60 mL) of dried oregano

4 bay leaves

2 teaspoons (10 mL) of salt

Lots of freshly ground pepper

FOR THE CHEESE SAUCE

4 eggs, beaten

8 cups (2 L) or so of grated mozzarella cheese

2 pounds (900 g) of ricotta cheese

2 cups (500 mL) of grated Parmigiano-Reggiano or other Parmesan cheese

1 cup (250 mL) of whipping cream

1 teaspoon (5 mL) of salt

Lots of freshly ground pepper

TO ASSEMBLE THE LASAGNA

2 boxes (12 ounces/375 g each) of ready-to-bake lasagna noodles

2 cups (500 mL) of grated Parmigiano-Reggiano or other Parmesan cheese

2 cups (500 mL) of grated mozzarella cheese

Position a rack toward the bottom of the oven so the lasagna will sit in the middle. Preheat your oven to 350°F (180°C). Turn on your convection fan if you have one. Lightly oil an extra-large baking pan or roasting pan.

Make the meat sauce. Generously splash vegetable oil into a large saucepan over medium-high heat. Toss in the onions and garlic and sauté until lightly brown, 4 or 5 minutes. Add the ground beef, sausage meat and 1 can of tomatoes for moisture. Stir vigorously until the meat is completely broken up and evenly mixed together. Add the remaining tomatoes, the chicken broth, oregano, bay leaves, salt and pepper. Briefly bring to a furious boil, then reduce the heat to a slow, steady simmer for a few minutes. Remove from the heat.

Make the cheese sauce by simply stirring all its ingredients together in a bowl.

Continued

Assemble the lasagna in the following order:

- 2 cups (500 mL) of the meat sauce
- ¼ of the noodles (8 or 9)
- ⅓ of the cheese sauce (about 3 cups/750 mL)
- ⅓ of the Parmesan
- ¼ of the noodles
- ½ of the meat sauce (about 8 cups/2 L)
- ¼ of the noodles
- ⅓ of the cheese sauce
- ⅓ of the Parmesan
- ¼ of the noodles
- ½ of the meat sauce
- ⅓ of the cheese sauce
- ⅓ of the Parmesan
- All of the mozzarella

Place one long sheet of foil over another one the same length. Fold over one long side by ½ inch (1 cm) or so and crimp tightly, then fold and crimp another ½ inch. Open up the two sheets into one larger one and tightly crease the center seam. Lightly oil one side and invert over the lasagna, crimping the edges to cover tightly. Bake for 1 hour. Uncover and bake until the top browns nicely and the noodles are tender, another 30 to 60 minutes. A paring knife should slide in easily and if wiggled from side to side, there should be no resistance from the noodles. Rest and firm the lasagna for at least 15 minutes before serving.

STORAGE TIP

Refrigerate: Tightly seal the meat sauce and cheese sauce separately and refrigerate within 30 minutes of cooking. Store for up to 4 days before finishing the lasagna. • Tightly seal the finished lasagna and refrigerate within 30 minutes of cooking. Store for up to 6 days before reheating.

Freeze: Portion the lasagna, tightly seal and freeze for up to 30 days. Reheat straight from the freezer or thaw in the refrigerator for 1 or 2 days before reheating. Tightly seal leftovers and store in the refrigerator for just a few days.

EXTRA-CRISPY CRUSTED MAC AND CHEESE

Every kid has a favorite mac and cheese, and mine always includes lots and lots of crispy crust. If you haven't made a homemade batch in a while, this is a good place to start. Make it ahead and leave it in the fridge for microwaved meals on the fly. Or instead of filling one large baking pan, fill a few smaller foil baking trays. Pour in the creamy pasta, top with the crust, tightly seal and freeze for many meals ahead. MAKES ENOUGH FOR 8 TO 10, EASILY DOUBLED IN A LARGER OR SECOND PAN

TODAY FOR TOMORROW Prepare the sauce and crust a few days in advance, ready to combine and bake (see Storage Tip). • Fully cook this dish now and reheat anytime during the next several days (see Storage Tip).

FOR THE CRUST

2 cups (500 mL) of panko or regular bread crumbs

1 cup (250 mL) of finely grated Parmigiano-Reggiano or other Parmesan cheese

Lots of freshly ground pepper

½ cup (125 mL) of butter, melted

FOR THE MAC AND CHEESE

1 pound (450 g) of penne or macaroni

2 tablespoons (30 mL) of butter

2 onions, chopped

4 garlic cloves, minced

1 teaspoon (5 mL) of fennel seeds

½ cup (125 mL) of all-purpose flour

4 cups (1 L) of whole milk

1 cup (250 mL) of whipping cream

2 tablespoons (30 mL) of Dijon mustard

1 tablespoon (15 mL) of paprika

1 teaspoon (5 mL) of your favorite hot sauce

1 pound (450 g) of grated cheddar cheese

4 raw spicy Italian sausages, thinly sliced

Position a rack toward the bottom of the oven so the mac and cheese can bake evenly in the middle. Preheat your oven to 350°F (180°C). Turn on your convection fan if you have one. Lightly oil a 13- × 9-inch (3.5 L) baking pan with nonstick spray.

Prepare the crust by mixing together the panko crumbs, Parmesan and pepper. Thoroughly toss with the melted butter until everything is evenly coated.

To start the mac and cheese, bring a large pot of salted water to a furious boil. Add the pasta and cook, stirring, until the pasta is al dente. Drain and return to the pot.

Meanwhile, toss the butter into a large pot or Dutch oven over medium-high heat. Swirl gently to melt it evenly, then add the onions, garlic and fennel seeds. Sauté until the onions are lightly browned, about 5 minutes. Evenly sprinkle the flour over the works, then stir it in well to make a thick paste. Whisking constantly, pour in the milk and cream, then gently stir as the sauce thickens, about 10 minutes. Stir in the mustard, paprika and hot sauce, then mix in the cheese and sausage. Pour the sauce over the hot, steamy noodles and stir the works together.

Pour the creamy mac and cheese into the prepared baking pan. Sprinkle evenly with the bread crumb crust. Bake until deliciously golden brown, crusty and bubbly, about 30 minutes.

STORAGE TIP

Refrigerate: Tightly seal the finished sauce and refrigerate within 30 minutes of cooking. Store for up to 4 days before finishing the dish. • Tightly seal the prepped crust and refrigerate for up to 4 days before cooking. • Tightly seal the finished mac and cheese and refrigerate within 30 minutes of cooking. Store for up to 6 days before reheating.

Freeze: Portion the finished dish, tightly seal and freeze for up to 30 days. Reheat straight from the freezer or thaw in the refrigerator for 1 or 2 days before reheating. Tightly seal leftovers and store in the refrigerator for just a few days.

GRANDMA'S POT STICKERS

I learned how to make these from my friend Tiffany, who learned them from her grandmother, who taught her that with experience comes finesse. At first your dumpling-wrapping technique may be a bit tentative (you may even have a few do-overs), but by the time you've finished you'll have mastered the basic technique. Many years and hundred of dumplings later, you may even master the classic pot sticker—a beautiful row of identical pleats with a stylish curve. For now, though, here's an easier and foolproof wrapping method that you can use straight away.   MAKES ABOUT 50 POT STICKERS, ENOUGH FOR 8 TO 12 MEALS OR SNACKS, EASILY DOUBLED

TODAY FOR TOMORROW   Prepare the dipping sauce up to a week in advance. • Prepare the filling for the dumplings a day or so in advance. • Stuff the dumplings and freeze for later (see Storage Tip). • Fully cook the dumplings now and reheat anytime during the next several days (see Storage Tip).

FOR THE DIPPING SAUCE

¼ cup (60 mL) of soy sauce

2 tablespoons (30 mL) of rice vinegar

2 tablespoons (30 mL) of honey

1 tablespoon (15 mL) of Sriracha or
   your favorite hot sauce

1 teaspoon (5 mL) of sesame oil

FOR THE DUMPLINGS

1 egg

2 green onions, thinly sliced

1 pound (450 g) of ground pork

2 tablespoons (30 mL) of soy sauce

1 tablespoon (15 mL) of grated
   frozen ginger

1 teaspoon (5 mL) of toasted
   sesame oil

Lots of freshly ground pepper

1 pound (450 g) of 3-inch (8 cm)
   round dumpling wrappers

A splash of cooking oil

Make the dipping sauce by simply stirring all its ingredients together in a festive dipping bowl.

Now make the filling. Lightly beat the egg in a large bowl. Add the green onions, ground pork, soy sauce, ginger, sesame oil and pepper. Mix until thoroughly combined.

Get set to wrap. Lightly dust a few baking sheets with flour. Have ready a small bowl of water and a dry towel for your fingers. Open the wrappers and cover with a moist cloth to prevent them from drying out as you come up to speed.

Lay a wrapper in your hand. Brush a bit of water around the outer edge with your finger or a pastry brush. Place a heaping teaspoon or so of the filling in the middle of the wrapper, then fold it in half to form a half-moon. Tightly pinch closed. Carefully fold 3 or 4 pleats into the curved edge to help the dumpling sit flat. Place the dumpling on a baking sheet with its pleated seam facing straight up. Repeat, gaining finesse and confidence as you go, until the wrappers and filling are used up.

To cook, heat a large nonstick skillet with a tight-fitting lid over medium-high heat. Add a splash of cooking oil. Carefully arrange the dumplings pleated side up in the pan and cook until a crispy, golden crust forms on their bottoms. Grab the pan's lid with one hand and ½ cup (125 mL) of water with the other. Pour in the water and slam on the lid, trapping the steam. Cook until the dumplings are cooked through, 2 to 3 minutes, a bit longer if they were frozen. Remove the lid and let any remaining water evaporate. Serve immediately with the dipping sauce.

STORAGE TIP

Refrigerate: Tightly seal the dipping sauce and refrigerate for up to 7 days. • Tightly seal the filling and refrigerate for up to 2 days. • These dumplings will dry out in the refrigerator, so cook them as soon as you shape them.

Freeze: Freeze the uncooked dumplings in a single layer on the floured baking sheets. Transfer to zip-top bags, tightly seal and store for up to 30 days. Cook from frozen. Tightly seal leftovers and store in the refrigerator for just a few days.

SLOW-ROASTED SAUSAGE, PEPPERS, TOMATOES AND PASTA

I'm always amazed at how much flavor a slow, patient roasting can add to a hastily assembled pan of ingredients. Minutes to prepare, an hour to roast—and a lifetime of tasty memories. MAKES 2 MEALS, ENOUGH FOR 4 EACH TIME, EASILY DOUBLED IN 2 PANS

TODAY FOR TOMORROW Prep this dish a day or so in advance, ready to pop into the oven. • Roast the sausage mixture now and refrigerate or freeze, ready to be reheated and combined with freshly cooked pasta (see Storage Tip).

Preheat your oven to 375°F (190°C). Turn on your convection fan if you have one.

For the sausage and peppers, in a large bowl, combine the sausages, red peppers, onions, tomatoes, garlic, fennel seeds, oregano, salt, pepper, red wine and olive oil. Mix everything well. Transfer to a large, deep baking pan or roasting pan. Roast for 1 hour, stirring every 20 minutes or so. If you have the time, keep cooking for another 15 minutes or so for even more browning and concentrated flavor.

Bring a large pot of salted water to a furious boil. Add the pasta and cook until al dente, 10 minutes or so. Drain and return to the pot. Add half of the sausage mixture directly from the oven, reserving the other half for another meal. Stir in the baby spinach and olives until the greens are wilted. Fill a round of bowls and, using a vegetable peeler, top each with lots of shaved Parmesan.

STORAGE TIP

Refrigerate: Tightly seal the sausage mixture and refrigerate within 30 minutes of cooking. Store for up to 6 days before reheating.

Freeze: Portion, tightly seal and freeze for up to 30 days. Reheat straight from the freezer or thaw in the refrigerator for 1 or 2 days before reheating. Tightly seal leftovers and store in the refrigerator for just a few days.

FOR THE ROAST SAUSAGE AND PEPPERS

5 or 6 Italian sausages, cut into bite-size chunks

4 red bell peppers, cut into bite-size pieces

4 onions, cut into large chunks

2 pints (1 L) of cherry tomatoes (or 8 ripe plum tomatoes, quartered)

Cloves from 2 heads of garlic, peeled and halved

2 tablespoons (30 mL) of fennel seeds

1 tablespoon (15 mL) of dried oregano

1 teaspoon (5 mL) of salt

Lots of freshly ground pepper

1 cup (250 mL) of red wine

2 tablespoons (30 mL) of extra virgin olive oil

TO FINISH EACH OF THE MEALS (FOR 4 SERVINGS)

1 pound (450 g) of your favorite pasta

Half of the Roast Sausage and Peppers mixture

A 5-ounce (142 g) bag of baby spinach or kale

1 cup (250 mL) of black olives, pitted and halved

A small chunk of Parmesan cheese

GUJARATI RED LENTIL DAL AND BASMATI

Every day, more people eat rice and dal than perhaps any other dish on the planet, especially in Gujarat, India's historically vegetarian state. While I was there I made authentic rice and dal with an expert cook who cooked it for her family every single day. I was thrilled to discover that I made mine the same way she did. (I did learn a few new flavor tricks, though!) We both knew it was an incredibly easy way to get a lot of big, bright, healthy flavor on the table in a hurry. Now you know too! MAKES ENOUGH FOR 4 TO 6, EASILY DOUBLED

TODAY FOR TOMORROW   Make the dal ahead (see Storage Tip). Reheat anytime during the next several days while you make a batch of basmati.

Make the rice. For the very best fluffy texture, soak the rice in plenty of cool water for 30 minutes. Drain, rinse and drain again. In a medium saucepan, bring the water and salt to a furious boil. Add the rice, cover and turn the heat down to low. Cook until the rice is tender and fluffy, 15 minutes. Reserve, covered.

Meanwhile, make the dal. Toss the butter into a large saucepan over medium-high heat, swirling and evenly melting it. Toss in the onion, chilies and curry powder; sauté, brightening the flavors, 2 or 3 minutes. Pour in the water. Stir in the lentils, brown sugar and salt. Briefly bring the works to a furious boil, then reduce the heat to a slow, steady simmer. Cook until the lentils are mushy, about 15 minutes. Remove from the heat and whisk into a smooth purée. Using the large holes on a box grater, grate in the tomatoes. Give it a stir and set aside if you need to wait for the rice.

To finish the dal, splash the oil into a small skillet or saucepan over medium heat. Add the spice seeds, stirring gently to awaken and brighten their flavors. Have a lid ready, because they'll crackle and pop. When they're lightly toasted and fragrant, stir them into the waiting dal. Ladle the works over spoonfuls of rice, nestle in a lime wedge and top with cilantro leaves.

STORAGE TIP

Refrigerate: Tightly seal the dal and refrigerate within 30 minutes of cooking. Store for up to 6 days before reheating.

Freeze: Portion, tightly seal and freeze for up to 30 days. Reheat straight from the freezer or thaw in the refrigerator for 1 or 2 days before reheating. Tightly seal leftovers and store for just a few days.

FOR THE RICE

2 cups (500 mL) of basmati rice

4 cups (1 L) of water

1 teaspoon (5 mL) of salt

FOR THE DAL

2 tablespoons (30 mL) of butter

1 large onion, finely chopped

1 or 2 green chilies, seeds removed, finely minced

1 tablespoon (15 mL) of curry powder

6 cups (1.5 L) of water

2 cups (500 mL) of red lentils

1 tablespoon (15 mL) of brown sugar

1 teaspoon (5 mL) of salt

2 ripe tomatoes

FOR THE FINISHING FLAVOR FLOURISH

2 tablespoons (30 mL) of vegetable oil

1 tablespoon (15 mL) of cumin seeds

1 tablespoon (15 mL) of mustard seeds

1 tablespoon (15 mL) of coriander seeds

1 tablespoon (15 mL) of fennel seeds

1 lime, cut into 6 or 8 wedges

A handful of fresh cilantro leaves

ROTISSERIE CHICKEN RICE

It's easy to stretch a store-bought roast chicken into two meals when you bulk it up with this delicious rice dish. These classic ingredients permeate the rice with lots of comforting flavor. One taste and your planned leftovers just might become tasty seconds! And of course, you can always roast your own chicken.

MAKES 2 MEALS, ENOUGH FOR 4 TO 6 EACH TIME, EASILY DOUBLED

TODAY FOR TOMORROW   Roast a chicken 2 or 3 days before you need it for this dish. • Prepare the dish with everything but the rice and refrigerate for up to 4 days before reheating and finishing with the rice (see Storage Tip).

¼ cup (60 mL) of butter

4 onions, chopped

4 carrots, chopped

4 celery stalks, chopped

4 garlic cloves, minced

2 cups (500 mL) of rice

4 cups (1 L) of Homemade Chicken Broth (page 201), a low-sodium store-bought substitute or water

1 rotisserie chicken, meat shredded into bite-size pieces

2 cups (500 mL) of frozen peas

Leaves from 8 sprigs of fresh thyme

2 bay leaves

1 teaspoon (5 mL) of salt

Lots of freshly ground pepper

Preheat your oven to 375°F (190°C). Turn on your convection fan if you have one.

Toss the butter into a large Dutch oven with a tight-fitting lid and set it over medium-high heat, swirling and melting. Add the onions, carrots, celery and garlic and cook, stirring, for 3 or 4 minutes. Stir in the rice, evenly coating it with butter. Pour in the broth and add the chicken, peas, thyme, bay leaves, salt and pepper. Briefly bring the works to a furious boil, then cover tightly and transfer to the oven. Bake until the rice has absorbed the broth and is tender, about 30 minutes. Remove the bay leaves.

STORAGE TIP

Refrigerate: Tightly seal the dish and refrigerate within 30 minutes of cooking. Store for up to 6 days before reheating.

Freeze: Portion, tightly seal and freeze for up to 30 days. Reheat straight from the freezer or thaw in the refrigerator for 1 or 2 days before reheating. Tightly seal leftovers and store for just a few days.

HONEY-SPICED ROAST TURKEY LEFTOVERS

Roast turkey is not just for special occasions. You can roast one just for leftovers—a big bird can easily make a week's worth of food. But first drop it in the tastiest brine ever—you'll be glad you did. Remember: it's all about the leftovers this time. Way more fun that way!

If you don't have a pot and a fridge big enough to brine your turkey in, clean a picnic cooler with soap and boiling water. Seal 6 or 8 freezer packs in resealable plastic bags and add them to the works before closing the lid. MAKES A MESS OF LEFTOVER SOUP AND SANDWICHES, ENOUGH FOR 4 TO 6 EACH TIME

TODAY FOR TOMORROW   Make the brine up to a week in advance. • Skip the turkey dinner madness altogether. Roast the turkey, cool it and carve off both breasts for sandwiches. Use one now and freeze the other. Shred the leg meat for the soup. Make the broth and reserve for a few days before making the soup. Prep the vegetables for the soup a day or two in advance (see Storage Tip).

THE HONEY-SPICED TURKEY BRINE

4 gallons (15 L) of water

4 cups (1 L) of kosher salt

4 cups (1 L) of honey

½ cup (125 mL) of your favorite hot sauce

12 lemons, halved

48 bay leaves

8 heads of garlic, cut in half through the equator

¼ cup (60 mL) of dried thyme

¼ cup (60 mL) of dried rosemary

FOR THE ROAST TURKEY

1 turkey (25 pounds/11 kg or so), defrosted for 5 to 7 days in your refrigerator

4 onions, peeled and halved

4 large carrots

4 celery stalks

FOR THE BROTH

The turkey carcass

A few aromatic vegetables and herbs: chopped onions, carrots, celery; bay leaves, fresh thyme and rosemary sprigs

FOR THE SOUP

The turkey broth

An equal volume of your favorite vegetables—fresh, frozen, green, root, leftover or otherwise—cut into bite-size pieces

1 cup (250 mL) of rice, grains or lentils

Handfuls of fresh thyme, tarragon or rosemary sprigs

First make the brine. Measure 1 gallon (3.8 L) of water and the remaining brine ingredients into a very large pot that will fit in your refrigerator. Briefly bring to a furious boil, then reduce the heat to a slow, steady simmer. Simmer for 10 minutes. Turn off the heat and add the remaining 3 gallons (11.2 L) water. Cover tightly, cool completely and for best flavor refrigerate overnight, even for a few days. Strain as best you can. Refrigerate thoroughly before using.

Submerge the turkey in the brine. Fit the pot into the refrigerator (or if it's cold enough, leave on the back porch) and let sit for 12 hours or so. After the soak, remove the turkey, rinse thoroughly with cold water and drain well. Discard the brine.

Preheat your oven to 400°F (200°C). Turn on your convection fan if you have one.   *Continued*

Spread the onions, carrots and celery in a large roasting pan. Perch the turkey on top. Roast for 1 hour, then—without opening the door—turn the oven down to 300°F (150°F) and continue roasting for another 3 hours or so. Check the bird's temperature, and continue roasting until a meat thermometer inserted in the thickest part of the leg and breast reads 170°F (75°C). Total roasting time works out to 12 to 15 minutes per pound (26 to 33 minutes per kilogram)—5 to 6 1/4 hours for a 25-pound turkey. Remove from the oven, tent with foil and rest for 30 minutes before slicing.

Carefully carve off the breasts for sandwiches—use one now and freeze the other. Carve off the legs and shred as much meat from them and the carcass as you can for the soup.

Make the broth. Put the carcass in a large pot and add your choice of aromatic vegetables and herbs and just enough water to cover the works, a gallon (3.8 L) or so. Simmer for 2 hours. Strain, discarding the solids. Rinse and wipe clean the pot and return the broth to it.

Make the soup. Add your favorite vegetables to the broth along with your choice of grain or legume and the reserved shredded turkey. Toss in half the herb sprigs. Simmer until the vegetables and grains are tender. Meanwhile, pull the leaves from the remaining herb sprigs and mince them. Fish out the whole herb sprigs and replace them with their minced brethren.

STORAGE TIP

Refrigerate: Tightly seal the sandwich meat and shredded soup meat and refrigerate within 30 minutes of cooking. Store for up to 4 days before using.

Freeze: Portion, tightly seal and freeze the extra sandwich meat, soup meat, simmered strained broth and/or finished soup for up to 30 days. Thaw slowly in the refrigerator. Tightly seal leftovers and store in the refrigerator for just a few days.

OVEN-FRIED CHICKEN

If you don't happen to have a deep-fryer, you don't have to go without full-on crispy chicken. The oven-frying method is so easy, and the crispy crunchy crust is beautifully flavored with standard-issue poultry seasoning. To make your own seasoning, blend 1 tablespoon (15 mL) each of dried sage, dried thyme and dried marjoram with 1 teaspoon (5 mL) each of nutmeg, salt and black pepper. MAKES 1 CHICKEN, ENOUGH FOR 4 TO 6, EASILY DOUBLED WHEN BAKED IN 2 BATCHES

TODAY FOR TOMORROW For lots of tangy flavor, soak the chicken pieces overnight in 4 cups (1 L) of buttermilk. • Bread the chicken the night before, covering it carefully so the crust doesn't fall off, and refrigerate. The crumbs will soften a bit, but you'll save time. • Fry the chicken now and enjoy cold for a few days (see Storage Tip).

Preheat your oven to 400°F (200°C). Turn on your convection fan if you have one.

Cut your chicken into 10 pieces (or have your butcher do it for you): 2 thighs, 2 drumsticks, 2 wings and 2 breasts each cut in half. Pour the oil into a large roasting or baking pan, covering the bottom with a thin film. Heat the pan in your oven.

Stir together the flour, salt and pepper in a bowl. Whisk the eggs in a second bowl. Stir together the panko, cornstarch and poultry seasoning in a third. Working with one chicken piece at a time, and keeping one hand wet and the other dry, dredge it in the flour, turning to evenly coat and shaking off the excess. Dip in the egg, turning, coating and draining. Gently roll in the bread crumbs, evenly coating.

When the roasting pan is sizzling hot, carefully fill it with the breaded chicken pieces skin side up. Generously spray the top of each piece with cooking spray. Bake until the chicken is crisp, golden and fragrant and a meat thermometer registers at least 165°F (74°C), about 45 minutes. Briefly blot the bottom of each piece with folded paper towel before serving.

1 large chicken or equivalent chicken pieces

½ cup (125 mL) or so of vegetable oil

1 cup (250 mL) of all-purpose flour

2 tablespoons (30 mL) of salt

Lots of freshly ground pepper

4 eggs

2 cups (500 mL) of panko crumbs

¼ cup (60 mL) of cornstarch

2 heaping tablespoons (35 mL) of poultry seasoning

STORAGE TIP

Refrigerate: Tightly seal the cooked chicken and refrigerate within 30 minutes of cooking. Store for up to 4 days before enjoying cold or reheating.

Freeze: Portion, tightly seal and freeze for up to 30 days. Reheat straight from the freezer or thaw in the refrigerator for 1 or 2 days before reheating. Tightly seal leftovers and store in the refrigerator for just a few days.

VIETNAMESE CHICKEN CURRY

Vietnamese curries are typically lighter than Indian or Thai curries, but are no less aromatic. This heartwarming stew is flavored with fragrant lemongrass, umami-packed fish sauce and hearty sweet potatoes, and gets its richness and silkiness from coconut milk. It's a versatile dish that can be served over rice or a bowl of rice noodles. I like it best with a crusty baguette, pieces ripped off and dunked into the spice-filled broth, soaking up every last golden drop. MAKES ENOUGH FOR 4 TO 6 BOWLS, EASILY DOUBLED

TODAY FOR TOMORROW   Make the broth in advance (see Storage Tip). • Prep the vegetables for the curry a day or two in advance. Refrigerate in a zip-top bag. • Fully cook this dish now and reheat anytime during the next several days (see Storage Tip).

FOR THE BROTH

2 or 3 stalks of lemongrass, trimmed

2 tablespoons (30 mL) of vegetable oil

1 large yellow onion, chopped

2 garlic cloves, minced

2 inches (5 cm) or so of unpeeled fresh ginger, sliced

¼ cup (60 mL) of fish sauce

1 tablespoon (15 mL) of sugar

1 tablespoon (15 mL) of Sriracha, sambal oelek or your favorite hot sauce

4 cups (1 L) of Homemade Chicken Broth (page 201), a low-sodium store-bought substitute or water

FOR THE CURRY

3 tablespoons (45 mL) of curry powder

2 tablespoons (30 mL) of cornstarch

1 tablespoon (15 mL) of sugar

½ teaspoon (2 mL) of salt

2 pounds (900 g) of boneless, skinless chicken thighs, cut into bite-size pieces

A few splashes of vegetable oil

2 large sweet potatoes, peeled and cut into bite-size cubes

2 carrots, cut into small cubes

A 14-ounce (400 mL) can of coconut milk with cream

TO GARNISH

A handful of fresh cilantro, chopped

2 green onions, thinly sliced

1 crusty baguette

Make the broth. Bruise the lemongrass with the side of your knife, then cut it into 3-inch (8 cm) pieces. Splash the oil into a soup pot over medium-high heat, then toss in the onion and garlic. Sauté until they're lightly browned, 2 or 3 minutes. Add the lemongrass, ginger, fish sauce, sugar, Sriracha and chicken broth. Briefly bring to a furious boil, then reduce the heat to a slow, steady simmer. Cover and simmer until the broth is aromatic, 30 minutes or so. Turn off the heat and rest while you carry on, or chill the works and reserve.

Make the curry. In a large bowl, whisk together the curry powder, cornstarch, sugar and salt. Add the chicken and toss until it's evenly coated. Pour a few splashes of oil into a Dutch oven or large pot over medium-high heat, enough to cover the bottom with a thin film. Using tongs, carefully add the chicken pieces. Patiently fry them until they're golden brown and crusty on both sides, 10 minutes or so.

Add all the broth. Briefly bring to a furious boil, then reduce the heat to a slow, steady simmer. Simmer, tenderizing the chicken, for 20 minutes or so. Add the sweet potatoes, carrots and coconut milk. Simmer until the veggies are tender, 20 minutes or so more. Ladle out bowlfuls and sprinkle with cilantro and green onions. Serve with crusty baguette for dipping.

STORAGE TIP

Refrigerate: Tightly seal the broth and refrigerate within 30 minutes of cooking. Store for up to 4 days before making the curry. • Tightly seal the curry and refrigerate within 30 minutes of cooking. Store for up to 6 days before reheating.

Freeze: Portion the broth or finished curry, tightly seal and freeze for up to 30 days. Reheat straight from the freezer or thaw in the refrigerator for 1 or 2 days before reheating. Tightly seal leftovers and store in the refrigerator for just a few days.

PUNJABI BUTTER CHICKEN

This is one of my favorite Indian dishes and an amazingly fragrant way to show off your very own garam masala spice blend. You earn a real flavor dividend when you invest the time to marinate the chicken overnight. The chicken not only tenderizes but also absorbs the aromatic flavors. Get ready for the applause! MAKES ENOUGH FOR 4 TO 6, EASILY DOUBLED

TODAY FOR TOMORROW   Blend the garam masala a week or so in advance. Store in an airtight container. • Marinate the chicken for up to 2 days. • Fully cook this dish now and reheat anytime during the next several days (see Storage Tip).

FOR THE GARAM MASALA

2 teaspoons (10 mL) of ground cumin

1 teaspoon (5 mL) of cinnamon

1 teaspoon (5 mL) of ground coriander

1 teaspoon (5 mL) of ground cardamom

1 teaspoon (5 mL) of pepper

½ teaspoon (2 mL) of ground cloves

½ teaspoon (2 mL) of nutmeg

FOR THE CHICKEN MARINADE

Half of your garam masala

1 cup (250 mL) of plain full-fat yogurt

1 to 2 inches (2.5 to 5 cm) of frozen ginger, grated

4 garlic cloves, grated, minced or mashed

The zest and juice of 1 lemon

1 teaspoon (5 mL) of salt

¼ teaspoon (1 mL) of cayenne pepper

2 pounds (900 g) of boneless, skinless chicken thighs, cut into bite-size pieces

TO FINISH THE DISH

½ cup (125 mL) of butter

1 large onion, finely chopped

Half of your garam masala

A 28-ounce (796 mL) can of crushed tomatoes

1 cup (250 mL) of whipping cream

For the garam masala, stir together all the ingredients.

To marinate the chicken, in a large stainless steel or glass bowl, whisk together half of the garam masala, the yogurt, ginger, garlic, lemon zest and juice, salt and cayenne until smooth. Add the chicken, tossing until evenly coated with the marinade. Seal tightly and refrigerate overnight or for a few days.

When you're ready to finish the dish, toss the butter into a Dutch oven or soup pot over medium-high heat, swirling it as it melts. Add the onion and remaining garam masala. Sauté until the onions lightly brown, 5 to 10 minutes. Add the chicken with its marinade and the tomatoes. Briefly bring to a furious boil, then reduce the heat to a slow, steady simmer. Cover and simmer, stirring occasionally, until the chicken is tender, 45 to 60 minutes. Stir in the cream. Serve with steaming-hot basmati rice (page 95).

STORAGE TIP

Refrigerate: Tightly seal the butter chicken and refrigerate within 30 minutes of cooking. Store for up to 6 days before reheating.

Freeze: Portion, tightly seal and freeze for up to 30 days. Reheat straight from the freezer or thaw in the refrigerator for 1 or 2 days before reheating. Tightly seal leftovers and store in the refrigerator for just a few days.

CHINESE-RESTAURANT CHICKEN

This recipe is so easy to make, you can make a batch of this classic "red-cooked" dish in the time it takes to have take-out delivered! The sauce is traditionally thickened with cornstarch, which can be a bit finicky. When you reheat a cornstarch-thickened sauce, it'll thin a bit, because the delicate cornstarch loses its grip. MAKES ENOUGH FOR 4 TO 6, EASILY DOUBLED

TODAY FOR TOMORROW   Braise the chicken ahead, but stop before thickening the sauce. Cool and store the chicken in the sauce (see Storage Tip). • Fully cook this dish now and reheat anytime during the next several days, knowing that the sauce will thin a bit (see Storage Tip).

Heat a Dutch oven or soup pot over medium-high heat. Splash in a shallow pool of oil. Working in batches, patiently and thoroughly brown the chicken on all sides, transferring it to a plate as it's cooked. Add the chicken broth, soy sauce, sugar, sambal oelek, green onions, ginger, garlic and star anise. Stir, scraping up any flavorful browned bits from the pot. Return the chicken and briefly bring the works to a furious boil, then reduce the heat to a slow, steady simmer. Cover and simmer until the chicken is tender and fragrant, 45 to 60 minutes.

Remove the chicken pieces to a medium bowl. Strain the broth into a saucepan, reserving the aromatic solids, and bring it to a simmer. Toss the aromatics with the chicken. Stir the cornstarch into the water until dissolved, then whisk it into the simmering broth until it thickens into a sauce, a minute or so. Whisk in the vinegar and sesame oil. Pour the sauce over the chicken, and sprinkle with green onions. Serve with steaming-hot rice.

STORAGE TIP

Refrigerate: Tightly seal the braised chicken—with or without the cornstarch in the sauce—and refrigerate within 30 minutes of cooking. Store for up to 4 days before reheating.

Freeze: Portion the braised chicken—without the cornstarch in the sauce—or the finished dish, tightly seal and freeze for up to 30 days. Reheat straight from the freezer or thaw in the refrigerator for 1 or 2 days before reheating. Tightly seal leftovers and store in the refrigerator for just a few days.

TO BRAISE THE CHICKEN

A few splashes of vegetable oil

8 chicken drumsticks or thighs or both

2 cups (500 mL) of Homemade Chicken Broth (page 201), a low-sodium store-bought substitute or water

3 tablespoons (45 mL) of soy sauce

1 tablespoon (15 mL) of sugar

1 tablespoon (15 mL) or so of sambal oelek or your favorite hot sauce

4 green onions, cut into 2-inch (5 cm) pieces

2 inches (5 cm) or so of thinly sliced fresh ginger

2 garlic cloves, smashed

3 or 4 whole star anise

TO FINISH THE SAUCE AND THE DISH

2 tablespoons (30 mL) of cornstarch

2 tablespoons (30 mL) of cold water

1 teaspoon (5 mL) of white wine vinegar or rice wine vinegar

1 teaspoon (5 mL) of toasted sesame oil

2 green onions, thinly sliced

PROSCIUTTO LEMON WRAPPED CHICKEN

This amazing little dish will become legendary at your table. And when that's the case, you can easily quadruple the recipe every once in a while. Fill your freezer with a month of ready-to-fly meals. MAKES 2 MEALS, ENOUGH FOR 4 EACH TIME

TODAY FOR TOMORROW Stuff and roll the chicken breasts in advance (see Storage Tip). • Fully cook this dish now and reheat anytime during the next several days (see Storage Tip).

Prepare to roll the chicken breasts. Line a baking sheet with parchment paper or foil. Make 8 equal piles of lemon slices, each with 4 sage leaves. Lay out the prosciutto slices, 2 at a time, slightly overlapped along one edge, forming a rough square. Working with one chicken breast at a time, slide it into a large resealable plastic bag and pound it with the bottom of a small pan or a rolling pin until it's at least half as thin as when you started. Season generously with the pepper. Cover with the lemon slices interspersed with sage leaves. Slightly tuck in any odd-shaped edges, then firmly roll into a pinwheel of sorts. Place the chicken log at one short end of the prosciutto slices and roll neatly and tightly once again. Place seam side down on the baking sheet.

Preheat your oven to 375°F (190°C). Turn on your convection fan if you have one.

Place the fresh or frozen chicken rolls in an ovenproof skillet and bake until a meat thermometer reads at least 165°F (74°C), 30 minutes or so from fresh, 45 minutes from frozen.

Transfer the chicken to a plate. For fancy presentation or family-style eating, slice each portion into thick pinwheels, showing off the lemon and sage within. Place the skillet over medium heat. Careful, the handle's hot! Toss in the butter, swirling and lightly browning it as far as you dare. Stir in the sage leaves and lemon zest to slow down the cooking, then add the lemon juice to stop it cold. Pour over the chicken and serve.

STORAGE TIP

Refrigerate: Tightly seal the rolled raw chicken and refrigerate immediately for just a day or two. • Tightly seal the cooked chicken and refrigerate within 30 minutes of cooking. Store for up to 2 days before reheating.

Freeze: Roll each of the stuffed chicken breasts tightly in an individual sandwich bag, seal and freeze for up to 30 days. Thaw in the refrigerator for 1 day before baking. • After baking, tightly seal leftovers and store in the refrigerator for just a few days.

FOR THE STUFFED CHICKEN

4 lemons, sliced as thinly as possible (skin and all, seeds removed)

32 fresh sage leaves

16 thin slices of prosciutto

8 boneless, skinless chicken breasts

Lots of freshly ground pepper

FOR THE FINISHING BROWN BUTTER FOR EACH MEAL (FOR 4 SERVINGS)

¼ cup (60 mL) of butter

Leaves from 2 sprigs of fresh sage, chopped

The zest and juice of 1 lemon

JERK WINGS

These wings are addictively spicy, mysteriously delicious and undeniably a great way to get a lot of party flavor together in a hurry. As everyone dives into these wings and starts licking their fingers, you can tell tales of how hard you worked for them. Tell them how you sacrificed so much to get the wings marinating on schedule. They'll respect your forethought, and you'll love the schedule-busting trick of a good make ahead rally! MAKES 24 FULL WINGS, ENOUGH FOR 6 TO 8, EASILY DOUBLED

TODAY FOR TOMORROW   Make the marinade ahead. • Marinate the wings ahead (see Storage Tip). • Fully cook this dish now and reheat anytime during the next several days (see Storage Tip).

2 large yellow onions, coarsely chopped

Cloves from 2 heads of garlic, peeled

2 or 3 habanero peppers, halved, seeds and stems removed

The zest and juice of 4 or 5 juicy limes

½ cup (125 mL) of soy sauce

¼ cup (60 mL) of vegetable oil

¼ cup (60 mL) of molasses

2 tablespoons (30 mL) of cornstarch

2 tablespoons (30 mL) of ground allspice

2 tablespoons (30 mL) of dried thyme

1 tablespoon (15 mL) of ground cumin

2 teaspoons (10 mL) of salt

24 whole or 48 split chicken wings

First marinate the wings. Pile everything except the wings into a blender or food processor and purée until smooth. Pour the marinade over the wings and stir well, thoroughly coating the wings. Marinate, covered and refrigerated, at least overnight or up to 4 days—the longer, the better.

When you're ready to roast the wings, preheat your oven to 350°F (180°C). Turn on your convection fan if you have one. Line a baking pan or two with parchment paper or foil.

Neatly arrange the wings in a single layer. Roast, without turning, until beautifully browned and tender, 45 to 60 minutes.

STORAGE TIP

Refrigerate: Tightly seal the marinade and refrigerate for up to 7 days. • Tightly seal the marinating wings and refrigerate for up to 4 days before cooking. • Tightly seal the cooked wings and refrigerate within 30 minutes of cooking. Store for up to 4 days before reheating.

Freeze: Tightly seal the marinated, uncooked wings and freeze for up to 30 days. Thaw in the refrigerator for 1 or 2 days before cooking. • Tightly seal leftovers and store in the refrigerator for just a few days.

COFFEE SPICE CRUSTED STEAK WITH CHIPOTLE CHIMICHURRI

Every cook is allowed a secret ingredient that's unexpected and deliciously mysterious. And it has to be head-smacking obvious once revealed. Ground coffee is your secret ingredient in this amazing steak spice. This rub is good for any steak occasion, so you may want to double the recipe as a great make ahead strategy. MAKES ENOUGH CHIMICHURRI FOR ONE MEAL AND MORE THAN A CUP (250 ML) OF SPICE RUB, ENOUGH FOR A FEW STEAK DINNERS, BOTH EASILY DOUBLED

TODAY FOR TOMORROW Make the spice rub and the chimichurri ahead (see Storage Tip).

FOR THE COFFEE SPICE RUB

2 tablespoons (30 mL) of cumin seeds

2 tablespoons (30 mL) of fennel seeds

1 tablespoon (15 mL) of black peppercorns

1 cup (250 mL) of freshly ground coffee

2 tablespoons (30 mL) of chili powder

1 tablespoon (15 mL) of salt

FOR THE STEAK SALAD

1 thick strip loin steak, about 16 ounces (450 g) and 2 to 3 inches (5 to 8 cm) thick

A splash of vegetable oil

6 or 8 big handfuls of baby arugula

FOR THE CHIPOTLE CHIMICHURRI

1 bunch of fresh parsley

1 bunch of fresh cilantro

4 garlic cloves, peeled

1 chipotle chili in adobo sauce

½ cup (125 mL) of olive oil

¼ cup (60 mL) of red wine vinegar

¼ cup (60 mL) of water

1 tablespoon (15 mL) of dried oregano (or 2 tablespoons/ 30 mL of fresh)

½ teaspoon (2 mL) of salt

Make the spice rub. Toast the cumin and fennel seeds in a small dry sauté pan, releasing their flavors. Let cool. Grind in a spice grinder along with the peppercorns. (If you don't have a spice grinder or a mortar and pestle, leave the spices whole and use freshly ground pepper.) Mix with the coffee, chili powder and salt.

Lightly oil both sides of the steak, then sprinkle generously with a third or so of the rub, turning and patting to help it adhere thoroughly and evenly. Rest for 1 hour at room temperature for the crust and flavor to develop.

Make the chimichurri. Simply cram all its ingredients into a blender or food processor and purée until smooth.

Preheat your grill or a large, heavy skillet. Grill or pan-fry the steak, turning frequently, gauging doneness until you're happy, 15 minutes or so for such a large steak to reach medium-rare. Transfer to a cutting board, lightly cover with foil and let rest for about 15 minutes while you open the wine and get the rest of dinner ready.

Mound the arugula in a bowl or on a plate and drape with lots of thinly sliced steak. Drizzle generously with the chimichurri.

STORAGE TIP

Room Temperature: Store the rub in an airtight container for up to a month.

Refrigerate: Tightly seal the chimichurri and refrigerate for up to 7 days.
• Tightly seal leftovers and store for just a few days.

EL PASO SHEPHERD'S PIE

A well-constructed shepherd's pie is a thing of beauty, all poised and ready to be enjoyed for days. This version is especially tasty. It's always nice when your dinner is packed with big, bright southwestern flavors and colors. An hour to make, a week to eat and a lifetime to remember. MAKES TWO 8-INCH (2 L) SQUARE PANS, ENOUGH FOR 4 TO 6 EACH TIME

TODAY FOR TOMORROW Assemble the dish now and refrigerate for up to 3 days before baking. • Fully cook this dish now and reheat anytime in the next several days (see Storage Tip).

Make the meat base first. Splash the oil into a large Dutch oven or soup pot over medium-high heat. Add the onions, red peppers, garlic, chili powder, cumin and oregano. Sauté for 3 or 4 minutes. Stir in the ground beef, tomatoes, beans, tomato paste, salt, hot sauce, Worcestershire sauce and corn. Bring the works to a slow, steady simmer, then continue to simmer until the meat is tender, 15 minutes or so. Divide evenly between two 8-inch (2 L) square baking pans.

Now make the potato crust. Bring a large pot of lightly salted water to a furious boil. Add the potatoes and adjust to a slow, steady simmer. Cook until tender, about 15 minutes. Drain, return to the pot and mash thoroughly. Stir in the milk, cheese, green onions and pepper. Spread evenly over the meat with a rubber spatula.

Preheat your oven to 400°F (200°C). Turn on your convection fan if you have one. Place the shepherd's pie on a baking sheet to contain the inevitable drips. Bake until hot, golden brown and bubbling, 20 to 30 minutes.

STORAGE TIP

Refrigerate: Tightly seal the cooked pie and refrigerate within 30 minutes of cooking. Store for up to 4 days before reheating.

Freeze: Portion the cooked pie, tightly seal and freeze for up to 30 days. Reheat straight from the freezer or thaw in the refrigerator for 1 or 2 days before reheating. Tightly seal leftovers and store in the refrigerator for just a few days.

FOR THE MEAT BASE

A splash or two of vegetable oil

2 onions, finely chopped

2 red bell peppers, finely diced

4 garlic cloves, minced

1 tablespoon (15 mL) of chili powder

1 tablespoon (15 mL) of ground cumin

1 tablespoon (15 mL) of ground oregano

2 pounds (900 g) of medium ground beef

A 28-ounce (796 mL) can of crushed tomatoes

A 19-ounce (540 mL) can of black or kidney beans, drained and well rinsed

A 5½-ounce (156 mL) can of tomato paste

2 teaspoons (10 mL) of salt

1 teaspoon (5 mL) of your favorite hot sauce

1 teaspoon (5 mL) of Worcestershire sauce

2 cups (500 mL) of frozen corn

FOR THE POTATO CRUST

4 pounds (1.8 kg) of russet potatoes (8 to 12), peeled and quartered

½ cup (125 mL) of milk

1 pound (450 g) of cheddar cheese, grated

4 green onions, thinly sliced

Lots of freshly ground pepper

KOREAN SHORT RIBS

Cooks all over the world crave luxuriously braised, meltingly tender beef short ribs. There are as many ways to cook up a batch as there are corners of the globe. All are delicious but few are as good as Korean style. If you can find the time to do one thing in advance for this dish, brown the meat. It's nice to be able to focus on this crucial step. It's your only shot at adding the rich, deep flavors that can only come from respectfully browned meat. MAKES ENOUGH FOR 6 TO 8, EASILY DOUBLED IN A BIG POT OR LARGE SLOW COOKER

TODAY FOR TOMORROW   Brown the ribs a few days in advance. • Prep the vegetables for the braise a few days in advance. Refrigerate tightly sealed in a zip-top bag. • Fully cook this dish now and reheat anytime during the next several days (see Storage Tip).

Rinse the ribs to remove any bits of bone and pat dry. Splash a puddle of oil into a large Dutch oven or heavy pot over medium-high heat. Working in batches, patiently and thoroughly brown the short ribs, transferring them to a plate as done. Listen to the heat. A sizzle is the sound of flavor. Too loud, though, and a sizzling pan becomes a smoking-burning pan.

Return all the browned ribs and any juices to the pan and add the onions, garlic, broth, sugar, soy sauce, sesame oil and hot sauce. Briefly bring the works to a furious boil, then reduce the heat to a slow, steady simmer. Simmer, covered, until the meat is glazed and incredibly tender, 2 maybe 2 1/2 hours.

Transfer the ribs to a serving platter. Coat with the sauce and sprinkle with sesame seeds and green onions. Serve with steamed rice.

STORAGE TIP

Refrigerate: Tightly seal the ribs and refrigerate within 30 minutes of cooking. Store for up to 6 days before reheating.

Freeze: Portion, tightly seal and freeze for up to 30 days. Reheat straight from the freezer or thaw in the refrigerator for 1 or 2 days before reheating. Tightly seal leftovers and store in the refrigerator for just a few days.

TO BRAISE THE RIBS

5 pounds (2.25 kg) of short ribs

A few splashes of vegetable oil

3 or 4 onions, thinly sliced

Cloves from 1 head of garlic, minced

3 to 4 cups (750 mL to 1 L) of real beef broth, a low-sodium store-bought substitute or water

½ cup (125 mL) of brown sugar

½ cup (125 mL) of dark soy sauce

2 tablespoons (30 mL) of sesame oil

1 tablespoon (15 mL) of your favorite hot sauce

TO FINISH THE RIBS

2 tablespoons (30 mL) of freshly toasted sesame seeds

4 or 5 green onions, sliced diagonally

BROWN SUGAR GLAZED HAM WITH RAISIN DRIPPINGS

A slowly roasted, patiently glazed and graciously presented ham is a real showstopper, something to be proud of, and a great way to get a whole lot of food together in a hurry. Stand by for lots of flavor with this recipe. If you run a busy sandwich operation out of your kitchen, consider baking a ham just for sandwiches. Not only will you save big, but you'll enjoy a rustic deliciousness that you just can't get any other way. If you're only making sandwiches with this ham, omit the raisins, bake with the glaze, cool, cut into 3 or 4 large chunks and freeze. MAKES 1 LARGE HAM, 8 TO 10 MEALS OR MORE WITH LEFTOVERS, ENOUGH FOR A LOT OF SANDWICHES, EASILY DOUBLED IF YOU HAVE A BIG ENOUGH OVEN

TODAY FOR TOMORROW Prepare the glaze a few days in advance. • Fully cook this ham now and reheat anytime during the next several days (see Storage Tip).

Preheat your oven to 325°F (160°C). Turn on your convection fan if you have one.

Stir the sugar, mustard and juice together in a small saucepan over medium-high heat. Briefly bring to a furious boil, then reduce the heat and simmer for a few minutes. Cool.

Tightly pile the raisins in the middle of a large baking dish or a roasting pan. Using a sharp knife, carefully score the fatty surface of the ham in a diamond pattern, cutting all the way through the fat and about $\frac{1}{2}$ inch (1 cm) into the meat beneath. Position the works flat (cut) side down over the raisins, nestling them under the ham. Pour about half of the glaze over the ham, thoroughly working it into the crevices with your fingers. Pierce the center of each diamond with a whole clove.

Place one long sheet of foil over another one the same length. Fold over one long side by $\frac{1}{2}$ inch (1 cm) or so and crimp tightly, then fold and crimp another $\frac{1}{2}$ inch. Open up the two sheets into one larger one and tightly crease the center seam. Cover the ham, crimping the edges tightly to seal. Bake the ham until it's tender, about 2 $\frac{1}{2}$ hours. Uncover and carefully pour the remaining glaze over the ham. Bake, uncovered, for another 5 minutes or so. Remove from the oven and spoon the accumulated juices and glaze back over the ham. Continue baking and basting until a rich, shiny glaze emerges, 15 minutes or so.

Rest the ham for 15 minutes or so before slicing. Stir the pan juices, drippings, scrapings and raisins together, forming a sauce of sorts. Add a splash of water if needed to help dissolve all the flavors. Spoon into a service bowl. Slice the ham and serve with the sauce.

1 cup (250 mL) of dark brown sugar

½ cup (125 mL) of Dijon mustard

½ cup (125 mL) of apple juice or any wine

1 cup (250 mL) of raisins

1 large bone-in ham (8 to 10 pounds/3.5 to 4.5 kg)

A handful of whole cloves

STORAGE TIP

Refrigerate: Tightly seal the ham and refrigerate within 30 minutes of cooking. Store for up to 6 days before reheating.

Freeze: Portion, tightly wrap, seal and freeze for up to 30 days. Reheat straight from the freezer or thaw in the refrigerator for 1 or 2 days before reheating. Tightly seal leftovers and store in the refrigerator for just a few days.

PAN-ROASTED PORK CHOPS WITH HONEY RIESLING GRAPES

It's just as easy to quickly sear pork chops for maximum flavor as it is to slowly bake them to keep them juicy. It's equally easy to build a delicious sauce from the pan remnants. The secret is all of the above in a two-step pan-roast. For a make ahead twist and a convenient way to come home to dinner, use your slow cooker: skip the browning step, neatly cram everything into the slow cooker (double the grapes and wine for added moisture, but reserve the thyme), set to any heat and walk away. Stir in the thyme at the last second, then serve. MAKES 4 CHOPS, EASILY DOUBLED

TODAY FOR TOMORROW   Prep the onions and grapes a few days in advance.

4 thick, meaty bone-in or boneless
   pork chops

½ teaspoon (2 mL) of salt

Lots of freshly ground pepper

A splash or two of vegetable oil

1 red onion, thinly sliced

2 cups (500 mL) of seedless
   red grapes

½ cup (125 mL) of Riesling or
   your favorite white wine

2 tablespoons (30 mL) of honey

1 tablespoon (15 mL) of white wine
   vinegar

Tender stems from 6 or 8 sprigs
   of fresh thyme, finely minced

Generously season the pork chops with salt and pepper.

Heat a large skillet with a tight-fitting lid over medium-high heat for a minute or two. Splash in enough vegetable oil to evenly cover the bottom of the pan. Vigorously sear the chops until they're golden brown and crusty on both sides, 2 or 3 minutes each side. The goal here is not to fully cook the meat but to add lots of brown flavor while the pan's temperature is still high. Toss in the onions and grapes. Turn the heat to its lowest setting, cover with the lid and cook for 5 minutes. Remove the chops to a plate and rest the meat while you quickly craft the sauce.

Increase the heat to medium-high and pour in the wine. Stirring gently, bring to a furious boil, quickly reducing the wine to sauce consistency. Stir in the honey, vinegar and thyme. Drench the pork chops and serve.

STORAGE TIP

Refrigerate: Tightly seal the pork chops with the sauce within 30 minutes of cooking and refrigerate for up to 6 days before reheating.

Freeze: Portion, tightly seal and freeze for up to 30 days. Thaw in the refrigerator for 1 or 2 days before reheating. Tightly seal leftovers and store in the refrigerator for just a few days.

ROAST PORK TENDERLOIN WITH BACON GRAVY

Nothing goes better with roast pork of any kind than gravy, especially if that gravy is made with bacon. You can easily crisp a few slices of bacon, then use the fat to anchor a smooth, tasty gravy. And you can easily make a batch of gravy days, even weeks, in advance. What could be simpler? MAKES ENOUGH FOR 4, EASILY DOUBLED

TODAY FOR TOMORROW   Make the gravy a few days in advance. • Fully cook this dish now and reheat anytime during the next several days (see Storage Tip).

FOR THE PORK

4 onions, thinly sliced

2 tablespoons (30 mL) of vegetable oil

1¼ teaspoons (6 mL) of salt, divided

Lots of freshly ground pepper

2 large pork tenderloins, trimmed of silverskin

FOR THE GRAVY

4 thick slices of bacon, cut into thin strips

2 tablespoons (30 mL) of all-purpose flour

1 cup (250 mL) of Homemade Chicken Broth (page 201), a low-sodium store-bought substitute or water

¼ cup (60 mL) of red wine

½ teaspoon (2 mL) of red wine vinegar

Tender stems from 6 or 8 sprigs of fresh thyme, minced

Preheat your oven to 450°F (230°C). Turn on your convection fan if you have one.

In a bowl, toss together the onions, oil, ¼ teaspoon (1 mL) of the salt and the pepper. Pile the onions in the middle of a 13- × 9-inch (3.5 L) baking or roasting pan, forming a bed for the pork. Season the pork with pepper and the remaining salt and rest it on the onions. Roast until the pork is tender and reaches an internal temperature of 145°F (65°C), about 30 minutes. Rest for a few minutes before slicing.

While the pork roasts, make the gravy. Toss the bacon and a big splash of water into a large nonstick skillet over medium-high heat. Cook until the bacon is fully browned and evenly crispy, 10 minutes or so. Stir in the flour, forming a thick paste of sorts with the bacon fat. Slowly pour in the chicken broth and whisk until you have a smooth, thick gravy. Stir in the wine, vinegar and thyme. If you prefer a thinner consistency, add a splash of broth or water.

Pile the onions on plates, top with a few slices of roast pork and drench with gravy.

STORAGE TIP

Refrigerate: Tightly seal the pork and gravy separately and refrigerate within 30 minutes of cooking. Store for up to 6 days before reheating.

Freeze: Portion the pork and gravy separately, tightly seal and freeze for up to 30 days. Thaw in the refrigerator for 1 or 2 days before reheating. Tightly seal leftovers and store in the refrigerator for just a few days.

SHRIMP AND SAUSAGE PAELLA

I tasted my way through the heart of Spain's traditional paella-making countryside and discovered that Spanish cooks prize simplicity, bold flavors and distinctive cookware as much as I do. This version of their national dish is my homage to their incredible cuisine. It's simple and tasty, and in case you don't have a true paella pan sitting on a campfire in the backyard, it's adapted to a standard pot. You can easily make a big batch on the weekend to set yourself up for a week of lunches or a month of flavorful freezer meals. Even though paella is traditionally enjoyed as soon as it's made, after a day or so you'll notice how much more vibrant and mature the already big-bold flavors of this paella become. MAKES ENOUGH FOR 6 TO 8 MEALS WITH LEFTOVERS, EASILY DOUBLED WITH A LARGE POT

TODAY FOR TOMORROW Prep the veggies a few days in advance. Refrigerate tightly sealed in separate zip-top bags. • Fully cook this dish now and reheat anytime during the next several days (see Storage Tip).

Preheat your oven to 350°F (180°C). Turn on your convection fan if you have one.

Cut half of one of the red peppers into long, thin strips and reserve for the garnish. Dice the rest of the peppers. Splash the oil into a large soup pot or Dutch oven over medium-high heat. Add the onions, garlic, paprika, saffron and chili flakes. Sauté for 3 or 4 minutes. Stir in the rice, diced red peppers, shrimp, sausage, chicken broth, rosemary sprigs, peas and salt. Briefly bring the works to a furious boil, then turn off the heat. Arrange the reserved red pepper strips in an attractive pinwheel pattern on top of the works. Cover and bake until the rice is tender, about 30 minutes.

STORAGE TIP

Refrigerate: Tightly seal the paella and refrigerate within 30 minutes of cooking. Store for up to 6 days before reheating.

Freeze: Portion, tightly seal and freeze for up to 30 days. Reheat straight from the freezer or thaw in the refrigerator for 1 or 2 days before reheating. Tightly seal leftovers and store in the refrigerator for just a few days.

2 red bell peppers

2 tablespoons (30 mL) of extra virgin olive oil

2 onions, finely chopped

4 to 6 garlic cloves, minced

1 tablespoon (15 mL) of paprika

½ teaspoon (2 mL) crammed with saffron threads

½ teaspoon (2 mL) of chili flakes

2 cups (500 mL) of medium-grain rice

1 pound (450 g) of shell-on shrimp, deveined

4 of your favorite rustic sausages, thickly sliced

3 cups (750 mL) of Homemade Chicken Broth (page 201), a low-sodium store-bought substitute or water

3 or 4 sprigs of fresh rosemary

2 cups (500 mL) of frozen peas

1 teaspoon (5 mL) of salt

SEAWEED SALMON WITH GINGERY EDAMAME

These showstopper salmon fillets look and taste amazing, yet they're easy to make. They may look dinner-party fancy, but roll up a batch and you'll know they're weeknight easy too! They're also perfect for a fill-the-freezer rally. Roll up a dozen or so at once and you're all set for many meals ahead. Just fire them in the oven straight from the freezer or give them 30 minutes or so on the counter to begin thawing. Either way, they'll take a bit longer to cook. After 20 minutes of bake time, cut a small slit with a paring knife to check whether they're cooked. MAKES ENOUGH FOR 4, EASILY DOUBLED

TODAY FOR TOMORROW   Prepare and roll the fresh salmon in advance (see Storage Tip). • Fully cook this dish now and reheat anytime during the next several days (see Storage Tip).

Preheat your oven to 350°F (180°C). Turn on your convection fan if you have one. Line a baking sheet with parchment paper or foil.

In a small bowl, stir the miso, sesame oil, sugar, ginger and vinegar into a thick paste. Lay the nori sheets on your work surface. Smear the miso paste all over the salmon, then neatly fold and roll the nori around the salmon, making a neat package. Arrange the bundles seam side down on the baking sheet. Bake until tender, 15 minutes or so (or 20 minutes from frozen).

While the salmon bakes, make the edamame. In a small pot, combine the edamame, ginger, water and soy sauce. Cover and simmer until the beans are tender, 5 minutes or so. Toward the end, uncover and finish evaporating most of the moisture. Remove from the heat and stir in the tomato. Serve the baked salmon with a spoonful of the gingery edamame.

STORAGE TIP

Refrigerator: Tightly seal the salmon bundles in individual sandwich bags and refrigerate for a day or two before baking.

Freeze: Tightly seal the uncooked salmon bundles in individual sandwich bags and freeze for up to 30 days. Thaw in the refrigerator for 1 day before baking.
• Tightly seal leftovers and store in the refrigerator for just a few days.

FOR THE SALMON

¼ cup (60 mL) of your favorite miso paste

2 tablespoons (30 mL) of sesame oil

1 tablespoon (15 mL) of sugar

1 tablespoon (15 mL) of grated frozen ginger

1 tablespoon (15 mL) of rice vinegar

2 nori seaweed sheets, cut in half

4 skinless salmon fillets (5 ounces/ 140 g or so each)

FOR THE EDAMAME

2 cups (500 mL) of frozen shelled edamame

1 inch (2.5 cm) or so of frozen ginger, grated

¼ cup (60 mL) of water

1 teaspoon (5 mL) of soy sauce

1 tomato, diced

ASIAN SALMON BURGERS
WITH MANGO GINGER SALSA

These burgers are packed with flavor, deceptively easy to make and seemingly too moist to hold together as they cook. Amazingly, they'll hold. Because they're made from fish, they're moist at first, but they'll firm up as they cook and then amaze your taste buds.   MAKES 4 BURGERS, EASILY DOUBLED

TODAY FOR TOMORROW   Make the salsa and the burgers in advance (see Storage Tip). • Fully cook this dish now and reheat anytime during the next several days (see Storage Tip).

FOR THE SALSA

2 mangoes, peeled and finely diced

2 green onions, thinly sliced

A handful of chopped tender fresh
   cilantro sprigs

¼ cup (60 mL) of chopped
   candied ginger

1 tablespoon (15 mL) of grated
   frozen ginger

1 tablespoon (15 mL) of fish sauce

The zest and juice of 1 lime

FOR THE SALMON PATTIES

1 pound (450 g) of fresh skinless
   salmon fillets, cubed

2 cups (500 mL) stuffed full of
   fresh cilantro leaves

¼ cup (60 mL) of minced red onion

¼ cup (60 mL) of grated frozen ginger

1 tablespoon (15 mL) of soy sauce

1 teaspoon (5 mL) of Sriracha sauce

A splash of vegetable oil

FOR THE BURGERS

4 of your favorite burger buns

Your favorite burger garnishes
   and toppings

Make the salsa. Simply toss all the ingredients together. You can serve it immediately, but salsas benefit from a day or two of resting to strengthen and smooth their flavors.

Make the salmon patties. Pile all the ingredients into a food processor. Pulse the works a few times until they start to come together—you don't want it too smooth, but chopped just enough so you can form 4 patties with your hands. The patties will seem fragile but they will firm up as they cook. Freeze, refrigerate or cook immediately.

You can bake, grill or pan-sear the burgers. Bake in a preheated 400°F (200°C) oven until firm, 20 minutes or so. Grill or pan-sear over medium-high heat with a splash of vegetable oil. Heat your burger buns if you like, and build your burgers with flair and flavor. Serve with the salsa.

STORAGE TIP

Refrigerate: The salsa can be refrigerated, tightly sealed, for up to 5 days.
• The uncooked burgers can be refrigerated, tightly sealed, for 1 day before cooking.

Freeze: Freeze the uncooked burgers on a parchment-lined tray until rock hard. Tightly seal the individual burgers and freeze for up to 30 days or so. Thaw on the counter for 15 minutes or so before cooking. Tightly seal leftovers and store in the refrigerator for just a few days.

YESTERDAY'S TOMATO SAFFRON BROTH, TODAY'S FISH

Spend time now to save time later. Make this classically flavored, intensely aromatic broth ahead and days later come home with the catch of the day. It's better to finish this broth with firm, fresh fish than to freeze it with the fish. Most cooked fish has a hard time with the freeze-thaw cycle and will flake into an unrecognizable mess. Instead, freeze the broth alone, then keep an eye out for fresh fish. MAKES ENOUGH BROTH FOR 4 TO 6 BOWLS, EASILY DOUBLED

TODAY FOR TOMORROW   Make the broth in advance (see Storage Tip). • Fully cook this dish now and reheat anytime during the next several days (see Storage Tip).

FOR THE BROTH

A splash of vegetable oil

1 fennel bulb, trimmed, cored and chopped

1 or 2 large onions, chopped

4 garlic cloves, minced

2 or 3 big pinches of saffron threads

2 tablespoons (30 mL) of fennel seeds

¼ teaspoon (1 mL) of chili flakes

A 28-ounce (796 mL) can of diced tomatoes

4 cups (1 L) of fish stock, Homemade Chicken Broth (page 201), a low-sodium store-bought substitute, another can of tomatoes or water

1 cup (250 mL) of your favorite white wine

2 or 3 bay leaves

TO FINISH ON THE DAY

1 to 2 pounds (450 to 900 g) of your favorite fresh fish, cut into large pieces

A few splashes of Pernod or other anise-flavored liqueur

Make the broth. Pour a splash or two of oil into a Dutch oven or soup pot over medium-high heat. Toss in the fennel, onions and garlic and sauté until the vegetables soften, 3 or 4 minutes. Add the saffron, fennel seeds and chili flakes and continue to cook for a minute or so. Add the tomatoes, stock, wine and bay leaves. Briefly bring the works to a furious boil, then reduce the heat to a slow, steady simmer. Simmer, uncovered, for 20 minutes.

When you're ready, finish with the fish. Bring the broth to a furious boil, reduce the heat to a slow, steady simmer and nestle in the fish. Cook, very gently stirring so you don't break up the fish too much, until the fish is cooked through and tender, 10 minutes or so. Ladle into bowls and top each with a generous splash of Pernod.

STORAGE TIP

Refrigerate: Tightly seal the broth and refrigerate within 30 minutes of cooking. Store for up to 4 days before reheating.

Freeze: Tightly seal the broth and freeze for up to 30 days. Thaw in the refrigerator for 1 or 2 days before reheating. Tightly seal leftovers and store in the refrigerator for just a few days.

A BAG OF FISH FLAVOR

The classics are back, and that's because they work. Cooks have been tightly sealing fish with steaming-hot flavor since fishing and cooking were invented. You can too. This is a super-simple way to fill your freezer with stand-by flavor, ready-to-go goodness and lots of lickety-split dinners.

When it comes to folding and crimping these packages, practice makes perfect. You may have to start over once or twice, but you'll figure it out quickly. MAKES ENOUGH FOR 8 MEALS, EASILY DOUBLED

TODAY FOR TOMORROW Combine the vegetable mixture in advance. Tightly seal and refrigerate for up to 3 days. • Bags with fish can be put together in advance (see Storage Tip). • Fully cook this dish now and reheat anytime during the next several days (see Storage Tip).

1 red onion, thinly sliced

16 sun-dried tomatoes, thinly sliced

The zest and juice of 1 lemon

1 pint (500 mL) of cherry tomatoes, each cut in half

1 cup (250 mL) of Kalamata olives, pitted and halved

A 19-ounce (540 mL) can of chickpeas, drained and well rinsed

A 14-ounce (398 mL) can of artichoke hearts, quartered

¼ cup (60 mL) of white wine

2 tablespoons (30 mL) of olive oil

1 tablespoon (15 mL) of dried oregano

½ teaspoon (2 mL) of salt

Lots of freshly ground pepper

8 portions of your favorite fresh or frozen fish or shellfish

Make the fish bags. Cut eight 15-inch (38 cm) squares of parchment paper. Fold each square in half. Draw the largest half-heart you can from the seam, filling the paper. Cut it out. Open into a full heart. Repeat until you have 8 large hearts.

Fill the fish bags. Put everything but the fish into a large bowl; stir and toss until evenly mixed. Spoon a tight pile of the mixture, ½ cup (125 mL) or so, in the middle of one half of each heart. Top with your choice of fish and then another ½ cup (125 mL) of the flavors. Fold over the other half of the heart. Starting at the heart's indent, fold and crimp an inch (2.5 cm) or more of the paper all the way around to the heart's bottom, forming a tight seal. Tightly twist the remaining tail and fold it under the works.

Preheat your oven to 350°F (180°C). Turn on your convection fan if you have one. Bake until the fish is tender, 30 minutes or so. Carefully open one package to check whether the fish is cooked.

STORAGE TIP

Refrigerate: Tightly seal the fish-filled bags and refrigerate for just 1 day before cooking.

Freeze: Place the fish-filled bags on a baking sheet and freeze overnight, then tightly seal and freeze for up to 30 days. Cook straight from the freezer or thaw in the refrigerator for 1 or 2 days before cooking. Tightly seal leftovers and store in the refrigerator for just a few days.

VEGETABLES, GRAINS AND SIDES

VEGETABLES, GRAINS AND SIDES RECIPES

A WHOLE HEAD OF ROASTED CAULIFLOWER WITH ROMESCO SAUCE

Normally cauliflower is about as exciting as plain white rice. Not anymore, though! Roast the whole head and serve it with one of the world's great condiments—piquant Spanish Romesco—and you just might find a new obsession. Romesco sauce is a wonderful make ahead addition to your repertoire. Its tangy spiciness complements many dishes, and it's an especially good sandwich spread. Roast cauliflower is a real flavor revelation too. Try it once and you'll crave it forever. If you find the time to roast a few heads in advance, you'll be poised to add it to stews, pastas, vegetable salads and soups. You can also refrigerate the cauliflower and serve it with the Romesco sauce as a crudité snack of sorts. MAKES 2 HEADS OF CAULIFLOWER AND 2½ CUPS (625 ML) OF ROMESCO SAUCE, ENOUGH FOR 6 TO 8 SIDES, EASILY DOUBLED

TODAY FOR TOMORROW   Core the cauliflower and refrigerate in a zip-top bag up to 4 days before roasting it. • Make the sauce ahead (see Storage Tip). • Fully cook this dish now and reheat anytime during the next several days (see Storage Tip).

Preheat your oven to 350°F (180°C). Turn on your convection fan if you have one. Line a baking sheet with parchment paper or foil. Core the cauliflower with a paring knife by cutting around the stem at a slight angle, creating an easily removable cone.

Generously rub the surface of the cauliflower with vegetable oil, then season with salt and pepper. Place on the baking sheet and roast until beautifully golden brown and tender, about 90 minutes. You'll know the cauliflower is cooked through when you can easily pierce it with a wooden skewer.

While the cauliflower roasts (or days in advance), make the Romesco. Pile all the ingredients into a food processor and purée until smooth and delicious. Serve with the cauliflower.

STORAGE TIP

Refrigerate: Tightly seal the Romesco sauce and refrigerate for up to 7 days. • Tightly seal leftovers and refrigerate within 30 minutes of cooking. Store for just a few days.

Freeze: Tightly seal the Romesco sauce and freeze for up to 30 days. Thaw in the refrigerator for 1 or 2 days. • Tightly seal leftovers and refrigerate for just a few days.

FOR THE ROAST CAULIFLOWER

2 heads of cauliflower

½ cup (125 mL) of vegetable oil

1 teaspoon (5 mL) of salt

Lots of freshly ground pepper

FOR THE ROMESCO SAUCE

2 roasted red peppers

2 garlic cloves, smashed

A handful of fresh parsley

1 cup (250 mL) of extra virgin olive oil

1 cup (250 mL) of unsalted roasted almonds

¼ cup (60 mL) of sherry vinegar or red wine vinegar

2 tablespoons (30 mL) of tomato paste

1 tablespoon (15 mL) of paprika

½ teaspoon (2 mL) of salt

¼ teaspoon (1 mL) of cayenne pepper

MEDITERRANEAN KALE

There are few foods as nutritionally dense as kale and few dishes as flavorfully dense as this one. The hearty dark green leaves easily match the big, bold flavors of garlic, black olives and sun-dried tomatoes. Spend some time on the weekend trimming and bagging kale and you'll be poised for success when the time comes to rush a dinner to the table. Healthy never tasted so good.   MAKES ENOUGH FOR 4 SIDES, EASILY DOUBLED

TODAY FOR TOMORROW   Prep the raw kale and refrigerate in a zip-top bag for several days. • Cook this dish now and reheat anytime during the next several days (see Storage Tip).

1 large bunch of kale

1 cup (250 mL) of water

The zest and juice of ½ lemon

4 garlic cloves, thinly sliced

1 teaspoon (5 mL) of salt

Lots of freshly ground pepper

8 to 12 oil-packed sun-dried
  tomatoes, thinly sliced

1 cup (250 mL) of Kalamata olives,
  pitted and halved

Prep the kale by cutting along either side of the tough center rib. Stack the ribs and slice as thinly as you can. Tear or cut the leaves into bite-size pieces.

Heat a soup pot with a tight-fitting lid over medium-high heat. Add the water, lemon zest and juice, garlic, salt, pepper and sliced kale stems. Briefly bring to a furious boil, then reduce the heat to a slow, steady simmer. Continue simmering as the tougher kale stems get a jump-start on softening, a minute or two. Stir in the tomatoes and olives, then add the kale leaves. Cover tightly and continue simmering until the kale is tender, 3 or 4 minutes.

STORAGE TIP

Refrigerate: Tightly seal leftovers and refrigerate within 30 minutes of cooking. Store for up to 4 days.

PAN-ROASTED BRUSSELS SPROUTS AND APPLES

Please allow me this forum to clearly, loudly and publicly declare my unabashed new love for the most reviled vegetable of my youth. Ever since I stumbled onto the unknown-to-my-mom technique of pan-roasting these little cruciferous wonders of flavor, my perspective has changed. From mushy terror to tasty and tender! MAKES ENOUGH FOR 6 TO 8 SIDES, EASILY DOUBLED

TODAY FOR TOMORROW Trim the Brussels sprouts as soon as you bring them home. Refrigerate in a zip-top bag for up to 5 days. • Fully cook this dish now and reheat anytime during the next several days (see Storage Tip).

Heat your favorite large skillet or sauté pan over medium-high heat. Splash in the oil, let it heat up a bit, and then add the sprouts. Sauté, shaking and shivering the works as the sprouts caramelize. Your goal here is not to cook them through but to brighten their color as you add lots of caramelized flavorful patches here and there.

Add the apple, water, vinegar, butter, salt and pepper. Lower the heat to a slow, steady simmer, cover and cook just until the sprouts are tender, about 5 minutes more.

STORAGE TIP

Refrigerate: Tightly seal leftovers and refrigerate within 30 minutes of cooking. Store for just a few days.

2 tablespoons (30 mL) of vegetable oil

2 pounds (900 g) of Brussels sprouts, trimmed of woody ends

1 apple, unpeeled, cored and finely diced

¼ cup (60 mL) of water

1 tablespoon (15 mL) of cider vinegar

1 tablespoon (15 mL) of butter

½ teaspoon (2 mL) of salt

Lots of freshly ground pepper

SLOW-ROASTED CHERRY TOMATOES, GRAPES AND PEARL ONIONS

It's so easy to just toss this simple dish together and let the oven do all the work. Slow, patient roasting transforms these ingredients into a delicious blend of complementary flavors. This is a tasty way to dress up any grilled meat or fish with a side dish that also acts as a sauce of sorts. MAKES ENOUGH FOR 4 TO 6 SIDES, EASILY DOUBLED

TODAY FOR TOMORROW Prepare this dish in advance, ready to pop in the oven when the time comes (see Storage Tip). • Fully cook this dish now and reheat anytime during the next several days (see Storage Tip).

Preheat your oven to 375°F (190°C). Turn on your convection fan if you have one.

Gently toss the works together in a large bowl or directly in a 13- × 9-inch (3.5 L) baking pan. Slowly roast until the garlic and onions are golden brown and the tomatoes and grapes wilt, about 1 hour.

STORAGE TIP

Refrigerate: Prep this dish, tightly seal and refrigerate for up to 3 days before roasting. • Tightly seal the finished dish and refrigerate within 30 minutes of cooking. Store for up to 5 days before reheating.

2 pints (1 L) of cherry tomatoes

2 pints (1 L) of seedless red or green grapes

Cloves from 2 heads of garlic, peeled

2 cups (500 mL) or so of peeled pearl onions

1 tablespoon (15 mL) of fennel seeds

1 tablespoon (15 mL) of extra virgin olive oil

½ teaspoon (2 mL) of salt

Lots of freshly ground pepper

SESAME CASHEW BOK CHOY

A warm salad is one of my family's favorite ways to enjoy green vegetables. Efficient too. You can easily toss together a jar of the strong, distinctive dressing ahead of time. At the last second, lightly steam your favorite greens and finish with a quick toss of premade flavor.

This sesame sauce is deliciously adaptive to many warm vegetable salads. Feel free to fill a mason jar with a quadruple batch poised for a quick tossing with any freshly steamed vegetables. MAKES ENOUGH FOR 2 MAINS OR 4 TO 6 SIDES, EASILY DOUBLED

TODAY FOR TOMORROW   Make the sesame sauce in advance (see Storage Tip).

¼ cup (60 mL) of water

4 or 5 garlic cloves, thinly sliced

2 pounds (900 g) of baby bok choy
  or other Asian cooking greens

¼ cup (60 mL) of tahini

2 tablespoons (30 mL) of soy sauce

1 teaspoon (5 mL) of sesame oil

The zest and juice of 1 lemon

1 cup (250 mL) of toasted cashews

2 tablespoons (30 mL) of
  sesame seeds

Heat your favorite large saucepan or soup pot with a tight-fitting lid over medium-high heat. Splash in the water and garlic. Briefly bring to a furious boil, then reduce the heat to a slow, steady simmer. Pack in the greens, cover and steam until tender, 5 minutes or so.

Meanwhile, whisk together the tahini, soy sauce, sesame oil, and lemon zest and juice. Pour the delicious sauce over the steaming-hot greens and stir in the cashews. Sprinkle with the sesame seeds.

STORAGE TIP

Refrigerate: Tightly seal the sesame sauce and refrigerate for up to 7 days.
• Tightly seal leftovers and refrigerate within 30 minutes of cooking. Store for up to 6 days before reheating.

HONEY THYME GLAZED ROOT VEGETABLES

People like to debate whether cooking is an art or a craft. This deeply delicious dish proves it's both. It requires some craft to soften tough, hard root vegetables. Then, the art—the honey and thyme that make it all worthwhile.

Next time you're invited to a dinner party, offer to bring along this side dish. It's a hearty anchor for the table and a solid base for any potluck. You can finish the works before you leave home or stop just before you add the sweet potatoes, then add those and glaze at your friends' place. MAKES ENOUGH FOR 6 TO 8 SIDE DISHES, EASILY DOUBLED, SHOULD BE DOUBLED, USE YOUR BIGGEST POT, MAKE LOTS, FREEZE SOME

TODAY FOR TOMORROW Prep the vegetables in advance. Refrigerate in a zip-top bag for up to 3 days. • Fully cook this dish now and reheat anytime during the next several days (see Storage Tip).

First the craft: Match a large saucepan or soup pot with a tight-fitting lid and set it over medium-high heat. Add the water, honey, butter, vinegar, salt and pepper. Briefly bring the works to a furious boil, then reduce the heat to a slow, steady simmer. Pile in the turnips, parsnips and carrots—not the sweet potatoes!—and stir vigorously to evenly coat them with flavor. Cover and simmer for 5 minutes. Stir in the sweet potato. Cover and cook, without stirring or you'll mash the sweet potato, until the veggies are tender, 10 to 15 minutes.

Now the art: Uncover the veggies, turn up the heat and reduce the cooking broth to an intense golden brown syrupy glaze. Shiver the pot along the way—no stirring!—to keep the veggies from sticking. Turn off the heat, sprinkle in the fresh thyme and stir or fold just enough to evenly coat the works with the thyme.

STORAGE TIP

Refrigerate: Tightly seal the vegetables and refrigerate within 30 minutes of cooking. Store for up to 6 days before reheating.

Freeze: Tightly seal the finished dish and freeze for up to 30 days. Reheat straight from the freezer or thaw in the refrigerator for 1 or 2 days before reheating. Tightly seal leftovers and store in the refrigerator for just a few days.

1 cup (250 mL) of water

½ cup (125 mL) of honey

¼ cup (60 mL) of butter

1 tablespoon (15 mL) of cider vinegar

½ teaspoon (2 mL) of salt

Lots of freshly ground pepper

2 large turnips, peeled and cut into large bite-size chunks

2 or 3 parsnips, peeled and cut into large bite-size chunks

2 or 3 carrots, peeled and cut into large bite-size chunks

1 large sweet potato, peeled and cut into large bite-size chunks

Tender stems of 12 fresh thyme sprigs, finely chopped

BACON CHEDDAR
STUFFED POTATOES

Stuff your freezer with stuffed potatoes. While you're at it, you might as well pack them with flavor too. Too easy—bacon! Once a month or so, gear up to double or triple this recipe. You'll be amazed at your efficiency and you'll love being poised for many meals to come. If you're freezing, mix all the cheddar into the works—it freezes easier. MAKES 8 SIDES, EASILY DOUBLED

TODAY FOR TOMORROW   Stuff these potatoes in advance, ready to finish in the microwave or oven when the time comes (see Storage Tip).

Preheat your oven to 400°F (200°C). Turn on your convection fan if you have one.

Bake the potatoes directly on the oven rack until they're tender, 45 minutes to an hour. Squeeze them carefully (they're hot) to judge doneness.

Meanwhile, toss the bacon and a big splash of water into a skillet over medium-high heat. Cook until the bacon is fully browned and evenly crispy, 10 minutes or so. Remove from the heat.

When the potatoes are cool enough to handle, slice them almost all the way through, end to end, leaving a hinge like a book. Scoop out most of the flesh into a large bowl, leaving behind a wall of flesh about 1/4 inch (5 mm) thick. Add two-thirds of the cheddar, the sour cream, green onions, salt, pepper and every last bit of flavor you can scrape out of the bacon pan. Mash the works together until evenly mixed. Spoon the mixture back into the potato skins.

Just before baking, top with the remaining cheese and bake until the cheese melts and the potatoes are heated through, 20 minutes or so, longer if baking from frozen.

8 large baking potatoes

8 slices of thick-cut bacon, cut into thin strips

3 cups (750 mL) of your favorite grated cheddar cheese

1 cup (250 mL) of sour cream

8 green onions, thinly sliced

½ teaspoon (2 mL) of salt

Lots of freshly ground pepper

STORAGE TIP

Refrigerate: Tightly seal the stuffed potatoes and refrigerate for up to 3 days before baking. • Tightly seal the baked potatoes and refrigerate within 30 minutes of cooking. Store for up to 3 days before reheating.

Freeze: Tightly seal and freeze for up to 30 days before baking. Bake straight from the freezer or thaw in the refrigerator for 1 or 2 days before baking. Tightly seal leftovers and store in the refrigerator for just a few days.

POTLUCK POTATOES
WITH PARMESAN CREAM

This is one of my favorite go-to dishes for potluck. The essential scalloped potatoes. The crowd pleaser. Guaranteed, because this version is packed with aromatic garlic and oregano.

Make ahead is an essential part of any professional kitchen. Every restaurant chef knows they can bake a batch of classic potatoes gratiné like this, cool them thoroughly, cut them into an array of fanciful shapes, and reheat them quickly to dress up the plate. At home that just means I make the full pan, serve half and save the other half for a few days downstream! MAKES A LARGE PAN, ENOUGH FOR 10 TO 12 SIDES, EASILY DOUBLED

TODAY FOR TOMORROW Prepare this dish in advance, ready to pop in the oven when the time comes (see Storage Tip).
• Fully cook this dish now and reheat anytime during the next several days (see Storage Tip).

½ cup (125 mL) of butter

8 garlic cloves, minced

1 tablespoon (15 mL) of dried oregano

½ cup (125 mL) of all-purpose flour

4 cups (1 L) of milk

2 cups (500 mL) of finely grated Parmigiano-Reggiano cheese

1 teaspoon (5 mL) of salt

10 or 12 large russet potatoes (5 pounds/2.25 kg or so), peeled and thinly sliced

Preheat your oven to 350°F (180°C). Turn on your convection fan if you have one. Lightly oil a 13- × 9-inch (3.5 L) baking pan.

Toss the butter into a large saucepan or soup pot over medium heat. Swirl, melt and sizzle. Toss in the garlic and sauté until sizzling, fragrant and lightly golden, 30 seconds or so. Stir in the oregano and turn off the heat. Sprinkle in the flour and stir the works into a paste.

Return to medium heat and slowly pour in the milk, whisking the sauce as it heats and thickens. Briefly bring to a furious boil, then reduce the heat to a slow, steady simmer. Whisk in the Parmesan and salt. Remove from the heat.

Stir the potatoes into the sauce, coating them evenly. Transfer them to the baking pan, nudging them into an even layer. Bake for 90 minutes, then begin checking doneness every 10 minutes or so. Bake until the potatoes are tender throughout and golden brown and the sauce is bubbly, reduced and thickened, up to 2 hours in total.

STORAGE TIP

Refrigerate: Tightly seal the prepared (but not baked) dish and refrigerate for up to 3 days. • Tightly seal leftovers and refrigerate within 30 minutes of cooking. Store for up to 6 days before reheating.

Freeze: Portion the baked dish, tightly seal and freeze for up to 30 days. Reheat straight from the freezer or thaw in the refrigerator for 1 or 2 days before reheating.

RED LENTIL FRITTERS WITH APPLE CUMIN RAITA

My kids think these are the best treasure from my lentil-hunting travels. I agree. They're delicious. As it turns out, lentils are an impressively easy way to make a great fritter, and these ones make a great meal with any salad. I use Canadian lentils—they're the world's best!

The longer the lentils soak, the smoother and easier they'll purée. The entire fritter batter may be made in advance too. It's a delicate batter, and if you find it too thin to form fritters, whisk in a bit of flour.   MAKES 20 OR SO LARGE FRITTERS AND ALMOST 2 CUPS (500 ML) OF SAUCE, ENOUGH FOR 4 MAINS OR 6 SIDES, EASILY DOUBLED

TODAY FOR TOMORROW   Make the raita and the fritter batter in advance (see Storage Tip). • Make the raita and fry the fritters now, then reheat the fritters anytime during the next several days (see Storage Tip).

FOR THE RAITA

1 cup (250 mL) of full-fat Greek yogurt

Leaves from 1 bunch of fresh mint, thinly sliced

The zest and juice of 1 lime

1 teaspoon (5 mL) of cumin seeds, toasted

½ teaspoon (2 mL) of salt

½ teaspoon (2 mL) or more of your favorite hot sauce

1 green apple, unpeeled

FOR THE FRITTERS

1 cup (250 mL) of red lentils

1 cup (250 mL) of water

½ teaspoon (2 mL) of salt

1 onion, chopped

1 or 2 inches (2.5 to 5 cm) of fresh ginger, peeled and finely minced

A handful of tender fresh cilantro sprigs

Vegetable oil for frying

Make the raita ahead. In a small bowl stir together the yogurt, mint, lime zest and juice, cumin seeds, salt and hot sauce. Coarsely grate the apple into the mixture and lightly toss until the apple is evenly coated.

Make the fritter batter. Stir the lentils, water and salt together, cover tightly and let soak for an hour or two—even overnight.

Transfer the works to a blender or food processor. Add the onion and purée until very smooth. Add the ginger and cilantro, then pulse just to stir the mixture together.

To fry the fritters, pour 2 or 3 inches (5 or 8 cm) of vegetable oil into a deep-fryer or a large pot over medium heat. Carefully bring to 365°F (185°C), using a deep-fat thermometer to accurately measure the temperature.

Using two spoons—the first to scoop, the second to release the batter—gently drop large dollops of the batter into the hot oil. Work in batches so you don't crowd the pan. Stir gently until the fritters are cooked through and lightly browned, 4 or 5 minutes. Drain briefly on paper towels as you ready the rest of the meal. Serve with dollops of the raita.

STORAGE TIP

Refrigerate: Tightly seal the raita and the fritter batter separately and refrigerate for up to 3 days before cooking. • Tightly seal leftovers and store in the refrigerator for just a few days.

MULLIGATAWNY QUINOA

The big, bold flavors of classic mulligatawny are alive and well in this dish, brightening the healthy quinoa. A tasty twist indeed! MAKES ENOUGH FOR 4 MAINS OR 6 TO 8 SIDES, EASILY DOUBLED

TODAY FOR TOMORROW   Fully cook this dish now and then reheat anytime during the next several days (see Storage Tip).

2 tablespoons (30 mL) of butter

1 large onion, chopped

1 tablespoon (15 mL) of
curry powder

1 unpeeled apple, cored
and finely diced

A 14-ounce (400 mL) can of
coconut milk

1 cup (250 mL) of water

1 cup (250 mL) of any color quinoa,
rinsed well and drained

1 cup (250 mL) of raisins

½ teaspoon (2 mL) of salt

Lots of freshly ground pepper

Heat a large saucepan over medium heat. Toss in the butter, swirling and melting. Add the onion and sauté until it sizzles and softens, 3 or 4 minutes. Sprinkle in the curry powder and stir, blooming and intensifying the flavors, a minute or two.

Stir in the apple, coconut milk, water, quinoa, raisins, salt and pepper. Briefly bring to a furious boil, then reduce the heat to a slow, steady simmer. Cover tightly and cook until the quinoa is tender, about 20 minutes. Turn off the heat and rest, covered, 10 minutes longer before serving.

STORAGE TIP

Refrigerate: Tightly seal leftovers and refrigerate within 30 minutes of cooking. Store for up to 6 days before reheating.

Freeze: Portion the cooked dish, tightly seal and freeze for up to 30 days. Reheat straight from the freezer or thaw in the refrigerator for 1 or 2 days before reheating.

GOAT CHEESE POLENTA WITH THYME-STEWED TOMATOES

Hosting a dinner party? Looking for an impressive anchor for an appetizer or a main course? Here it is. Freshly made cheesy polenta is so delicious that it's hard to believe it could taste any better. But it can! Here's the deal. Pour fresh polenta into a loaf pan and cool into firm, easily sliceable, easily crisped leftovers, ready to be sauced with simply stewed tomatoes. All the more impressive when made in advance. MAKES A LARGE LOAF, ENOUGH FOR 8 TO 12 SIDES, EASILY DOUBLED IN 2 PANS

TODAY FOR TOMORROW   Make the polenta loaf in advance, ready to slice and crisp when ready to eat (see Storage Tip).
• Stew the tomatoes a few days in advance, ready to reheat briefly (see Storage Tip).

FOR THE POLENTA LOAF

¼ cup (60 mL) of butter

2 onions, chopped

8 garlic cloves, finely minced

8 cups (2 L) of milk, Homemade
  Chicken Broth (page 201),
  a low-sodium store-bought
  substitute, water
  or any mixture of these

1 teaspoon (5 mL) of salt

Lots of freshly ground pepper

2 cups (500 mL) of cornmeal

8 to 10 ounces (225 to 280 g)
  of goat cheese, crumbled

1 cup (250 mL) of chopped
  fresh parsley

FOR THE STEWED TOMATOES

¼ cup (60 mL) of butter

2 onions, chopped

4 garlic cloves, thinly sliced

2 pints (1 L) of cherry tomatoes,
  halved

2 tablespoons (30 mL) of
  red wine vinegar

½ teaspoon (2 mL) of salt

Lots of freshly ground pepper

Tender stems from 12 sprigs
  of fresh thyme, finely chopped

FOR FRYING THE POLENTA SLICES

A few splashes of vegetable oil

A spoonful or two of butter

A handful or two of all-purpose flour

Make the polenta loaf. Lightly oil a large loaf pan. Toss the butter into a large saucepan or soup pot over medium heat, swirling and melting. Add the onions and garlic and sauté until they soften, 2 or 3 minutes. Pour in your liquid choice and add the salt and pepper. Briefly bring to a furious boil, then reduce the heat to a slow, steady simmer. Whisking constantly to prevent lumps, slowly pour in the cornmeal. Switch to a wooden spoon and continue simmering, stirring frequently, until the cornmeal absorbs all the liquid and a thick, smooth polenta forms, 10 minutes or so. Stir in the goat cheese and parsley. Pour the works into the loaf pan and evenly smooth the top. Tightly wrap, pressing plastic wrap directly on the surface of the polenta, and refrigerate overnight.

Stew the tomatoes. Melt the butter in a small sauté pan or skillet. Toss in the onions and garlic and sauté briefly, until lightly browned and fragrant. Add the tomatoes, vinegar, salt and pepper and continue cooking until the tomatoes simmer and soften into a tasty stew, a minute or two. Turn off the heat and stir in the thyme.

Fry the polenta. Turn the polenta loaf out of the pan and cut into slices an inch (2.5 cm) or so thick. Heat a heavy skillet over medium-high heat. Splash in the vegetable oil and add the butter. Dredge the polenta slices in flour, shaking off the excess, and gently fry in the sizzling butter, turning occasionally, until golden brown on both sides. Serve with the stewed tomatoes.

STORAGE TIP

Refrigerate: Tightly seal the polenta and refrigerate within 30 minutes of cooking. Store for up to 5 days before slicing and crisping. • Tightly seal the tomatoes and refrigerate within 30 minutes of cooking. Store for up to 5 days.

Freeze: Tightly seal the polenta—sliced or unsliced—and freeze for up to 30 days. Reheat straight from the freezer or thaw in the refrigerator for a day before reheating. Tightly seal leftovers and store in the refrigerator for just a few days.

BROWN RICE AND LENTILS

This tasty side dish is a hearty way to bring lots of healthy protein to your table while lightening the load at checkout. Meat is a great source of protein, but lentils are a tasty and less expensive alternative. This dish is great served chilled. MAKES ENOUGH FOR 4 MAINS OR 6 TO 8 SIDES, EASILY DOUBLED

TODAY FOR TOMORROW Prep the onion and garlic a few days in advance, ready to toss in the pan when the time comes. Refrigerate tightly sealed in a zip-top bag. • Fully cook this dish now and reheat anytime during the next several days (see Storage Tip).

Heat a large saucepan over medium-high heat. Splash in the vegetable oil, then toss in the onion and garlic. Sauté for 2 or 3 minutes. Add the rice, lentils, chicken broth, bay leaf, salt and pepper. Briefly bring to a furious boil, then reduce the heat to a slow, steady simmer. Cover tightly and simmer until the lentils and rice are tender, 45 minutes or so. Turn off the heat and let rest, covered, for a few minutes.

STORAGE TIP

Refrigerate: Tightly seal leftovers and refrigerate within 30 minutes of cooking. Store for up to 6 days before reheating.

Freeze: Portion, tightly seal and freeze for up to 30 days. Reheat straight from the freezer or thaw in the refrigerator for 1 or 2 days before reheating. Tightly seal leftovers and store in the refrigerator for just a few days.

A splash of vegetable oil

1 large onion, minced

4 garlic cloves, minced

1 cup (250 mL) of brown rice

1 cup (250 mL) of brown or
    green lentils

4 cups (1 L) of Homemade Chicken
    Broth (page 201), a low-sodium
    store-bought substitute or water

A bay leaf or two

1 teaspoon (5 mL) of salt

Lots of freshly ground pepper

READY TO GO

READY TO GO RECIPES

SAN MARZANO MARINARA SAUCE

Authenticity is a bold claim, but this sauce delivers with two key ingredients—great tomatoes and speed. Turns out the secret to a great marinara sauce—the classic sauce that captures the flavor of the Italian sun—is speed, not a lengthy simmer. A brief heating unlocks that fresh tomato taste and locks in peak flavor. The true flavor of a field-ripe sun-warmed tomato only fades with time. You can make this sauce faster than you can drive to the store and buy it! MAKES 3 QUARTS (3 L), ENOUGH FOR 3 GIANT PASTA FEEDS, EASILY DOUBLED IN A MUCH LARGER POT

TODAY FOR TOMORROW Prepare this sauce ahead, ready to toss into a batch of pasta or another dish when the time comes (see Storage Tip). • Use your prepared sauce for the recipes that follow: Pan-Roasted Chicken (page 171), Old-School Baked Meatball Subs (page 172), Slow-Baked Chicken (page 175).

Splash the oil into a large saucepan or soup pot over medium heat. Toss in the garlic cloves and gently stir and fry long enough to fully release their pungent flavors into the oil, just a minute or so. Stir in the oregano, salt and chili flakes. Turn off the heat while you add the tomatoes.

Open each can of preserved sunshine and pour through your fingers into the pot, crushing the tomatoes with your hand into smaller, rustic pieces. Swirl the cup of water through each successive can, then into the pot. Briefly bring the works to a furious boil, then reduce the heat to a slow, steady simmer. Cook just long enough to release the tomatoes' flavors and soften their texture, 15 minutes or so.

Pour into sterile mason jars, nearly filling them. Place the lids tightly on the jars and loosely screw on the collars, halfway or so. Rest the jars on the counter until the lids pop down, 30 minutes or so, then tightly screw the collars down. As the sauce cools it will shrink, contract and pull the lids even tighter. Refrigerate for up to a month or so, but it's doubtful it will last that long.

½ cup (125 mL) of your very best extra virgin olive oil

Cloves from 2 heads of garlic, peeled and smashed

1 tablespoon (15 mL) of dried oregano

1 teaspoon (5 mL) of salt

¼ teaspoon (1 mL) of chili flakes

4 cans (28 ounces/796 mL each) of whole Roma tomatoes, preferably San Marzano

1 cup (250 mL) of water

STORAGE TIP

Refrigerate: Tightly seal the sauce and refrigerate for up to 4 weeks before reheating.

Freeze: Portion, tightly seal and freeze for up to 30 days. Reheat straight from the freezer or thaw in the refrigerator for 1 or 2 days before reheating. Tightly seal leftovers and store in the refrigerator for just a few days.

PAN-ROASTED CHICKEN WITH STEAMING PASTA, SAN MARZANO MARINARA AND WILTED SPINACH

There are many ways to leverage a jar of bright marinara sauce into a memorable meal. This basic four-part method is one of the best. It's a reliable way to quickly craft a fully balanced meal. A jar of sauce, any just-seared meat, steaming noodles, wilted fresh greens—you can make dinner in the time it takes you to boil water and cook pasta.

This dish's formula can be spun into so many varied meals. The chicken can easily become beefy steak, juicy pork tenderloin, lamb, bacon, salmon, scallops or catch of the day. And in place of spinach, you have the universe of green vegetables to choose from. MAKES ENOUGH FOR 6 TO 8, EASILY DOUBLED

TODAY FOR TOMORROW   Make the San Marzano Marinara Sauce ahead. • If you're using a vegetable other than greens, trim and prep it a few days ahead. Refrigerate in a zip-top bag. • Fully cook this dish now and reheat anytime during the next several days (see Storage Tip).

Bring a large pot of salted water to a boil.

Heat a heavy skillet or large sauté pan over medium-high heat and splash in a pool of vegetable oil. Generously season the chicken breasts with salt and pepper. Using tongs, carefully add the chicken to the sizzling pan, cover and pan-roast, turning occasionally, until browned and tender, 15 minutes or so. Transfer the chicken to a plate and rest for 10 minutes or so.

Meanwhile, add the pasta to the boiling water and cook until it's al dente, 10 minutes or so.

Also meanwhile, pour the marinara sauce into the sauté pan and bring to a slow, steady simmer, stirring to dissolve the bits of caramelized flavor. Slice the chicken and return it to the pan. Cover, turn off the heat and rest a few minutes as you finish up the pasta.

Drain the pasta and quickly return the proceeds to the pot. Top with a thick layer of greens, then top with the simmering tomato chicken mixture. Stir everything together and cover tightly. Rest for a few minutes as the greens finish wilting.

A few splashes of vegetable oil

2 to 4 boneless, skinless chicken breasts

1 teaspoon (5 mL) or so of salt

Lots of freshly ground pepper

1 pound (450 g) of your favorite pasta

2 to 4 cups (500 mL to 1 L) of San Marzano Marinara Sauce (page 169)

1 large container (11 ounces/312 g) of baby spinach, kale or other baby greens

STORAGE TIP

Refrigerate: Tightly seal leftovers and refrigerate within 30 minutes of cooking. Store for up to 4 days before reheating.

OLD-SCHOOL BAKED MEATBALL SUBS

Life's too short not to tuck into a crusty, cheesy, hot baked sub now and then, especially this bit of classic culinary genius. Crispy golden buns full of freshly sauced meatballs topped with cheesy goodness—it's only made better by making it yourself. MAKES 24 LARGE MEATBALLS, ENOUGH FOR 8 BAKED SUBS

TODAY FOR TOMORROW Make the San Marzano Marinara Sauce ahead. • Prepare the meatballs—browned or not—in advance (see Storage Tip).

FOR THE MEATBALLS

½ cup (125 mL) of plain dry bread crumbs

4 ounces (115 g) of Parmigiano-Reggiano cheese, broken into small pieces

½ cup (125 mL) of milk

1 onion, finely chopped

4 garlic cloves, peeled and smashed

A handful of fresh parsley leaves, torn

1 egg, lightly beaten

1 tablespoon (15 mL) of dried oregano

1 teaspoon (5 mL) of salt

Lots of freshly ground pepper

2 pounds (900 g) of medium ground beef

FOR EACH SUB

A freshly baked crusty sub bun

6 or 8 fresh basil leaves

¼ cup (60 mL) of San Marzano Marinara Sauce (page 169)

A handful of grated mozzarella cheese

Make the meatballs. Position a rack near the top of the oven and preheat your broiler. Turn on your convection fan if you have one. Line a pair of baking sheets with foil or parchment paper.

In a food processor, pulse the bread crumbs and Parmesan, breaking the cheese down into the bread crumbs. Splash in the milk and briefly pulse. Rest for 10 minutes as the bread absorbs the moisture, ensuring juicy meatballs ahead.

Add the onion, garlic and parsley, and pulse until thoroughly mixed into a smooth paste. Add the egg, oregano, salt and pepper; pulse just enough to mix. Toss the meat into a large bowl, and using your hands, break it down into smaller chunks. Add every drop of the egg mixture and mix thoroughly into a smooth, firm mixture. Divide into 24 equal pieces and shape each piece into a 2-inch (5 cm) meatball. Arrange neatly on the baking sheets.

To cook, broil, turning once, just long enough to brown them thoroughly and cook them through without drying them out, 10 minutes or so. Remove them from the oven and set aside. Set the oven to 400°F (200°C).

Meanwhile, cut deeply through the top of each bun, leaving a strong hinge. Neatly stuff with fresh basil leaves and top with 3 seared meatballs. Cover with marinara sauce, then evenly cover with mozzarella cheese. Carefully nestle the subs into a baking dish that keeps them upright. Bake on the top rack until steaming hot and browned, 15 to 20 minutes.

STORAGE TIP

Refrigerate: Tightly seal the browned meatballs and refrigerate within 30 minutes of cooking. Store for up to 3 days before baking in the buns.

Freeze: Freeze the raw or browned meatballs on the baking sheets until rock hard. Tightly seal and freeze for up to 30 days. Cook or reheat straight from the freezer or thaw in the refrigerator for 1 or 2 days before cooking or reheating. Tightly seal leftovers and store in the refrigerator for a day or two before reheating.

SLOW-BAKED CHICKEN WITH SAN MARZANO MARINARA, OLIVES AND OREGANO RICE

This dish is a great way to spin a bottle of fresh tomato sauce into a simple, hearty meal. Braise chicken thighs in your own simmering marinara sauce and bring lots of other fresh Mediterranean flavors along for the ride too! Don't feel you'll be missing something by not browning the meat. The long, slow cooking triggers a lower-heat browning just as packed with deep flavor.   MAKES ENOUGH FOR 4 TO 6 MAINS, EASILY DOUBLED

TODAY FOR TOMORROW   Make the San Marzano Marinara Sauce ahead. • Prep the onions, garlic and olives a few days ahead. Refrigerate tightly sealed in a zip-top bag. • Cook the chicken in advance, ready to reheat when you make the rice (see Storage Tip). • Fully cook both the chicken and the rice now and reheat anytime during the next several days (see Storage Tip).

Begin by baking the chicken. Preheat your oven to 350°F (180°C). Turn on your convection fan if you have one.

Match a large ovenproof skillet with a tight-fitting lid and set it over medium-high heat. Fill it with the onions, garlic and olives. Stir in the marinara sauce and nestle in the chicken pieces. Briefly bring the works to a furious boil, then reduce the heat to a slow, steady simmer. Cover tightly, transfer to the oven and bake until the chicken is so tender that you can tug out any bones, an hour and 15 minutes or so.

Meanwhile, make the rice. In a medium saucepan, combine the water, rice, butter, oregano, salt and pepper. Briefly bring to a furious boil over medium-high heat, then reduce the heat to a slow, steady simmer. Cover tightly and cook—without lifting the lid—until the rice is tender and moist, 15 minutes or so. Turn off the heat and rest, tightly covered, for 5 minutes or longer before serving.

STORAGE TIP

Refrigerate: Tightly seal the chicken and refrigerate within 30 minutes of cooking. Store for up to 4 days before reheating.

Freeze: Tightly seal the cooked dish with the rice and freeze for up to 30 days. Reheat straight from the freezer or thaw in the refrigerator for a day or so before reheating.

FOR THE CHICKEN

2 onions, thinly sliced

4 garlic cloves, thinly sliced

1 cup (250 mL) or so of your favorite Kalamata-style olives, pitted

2 cups (500 mL) of San Marzano Marinara Sauce (page 169)

6 or 8 chicken thighs or drumsticks, or 4 breasts, boneless and skinless or not

FOR THE RICE

2 cups (500 mL) of water

1 cup (250 mL) of any white rice

A tablespoon (15 mL) or two of butter

Leaves from a few sprigs of fresh oregano or rosemary, finely minced

1 teaspoon (5 mL) of salt

Lots of freshly ground pepper

SPICY GREEN PESTO

Pesto is an intensely flavored condiment traditionally made from fresh green herbs, nuts, cheese and olive oil. It's an incredibly easy way to add a big, bright boost of fresh flavor to nearly any dish. This version is less expensive than the classic Genovese blend of basil, pine nuts and Parmigiano-Reggiano, but with spicy arugula, peperoncini and almonds it's just as flavorful. You can just as easily incorporate traditional fresh basil into the works if you like. Either way, you'll discover that a little goes a long way. MAKES 2 CUPS (500 ML), ENOUGH FOR MANY MEALS, EASILY DOUBLED

TODAY FOR TOMORROW Make this pesto ahead (see Storage Tip). • Use your prepared pesto for the recipes that follow: Pan-Roasted Chicken (page 179), Pan-Baked Salmon (page 180), Penne with Green Veggies (page 183).

Pile the garlic, peperoncini, almonds and half of the olive oil into your food processor. Pulse until everything is coarsely chopped and well mixed. Add the remaining oil and the Parmesan, arugula, salt and pepper. Process, scraping down the sides occasionally, until thoroughly blended into a smooth paste.

STORAGE TIP

Refrigerate: Tightly seal the pesto and refrigerate for up to a week.

Freeze: Portion the pesto, tightly seal and freeze for up to 30 days. Use straight from the freezer or thaw in the refrigerator for a day or so before use.

2 garlic cloves, peeled

2 pickled peperoncini peppers, stems removed (or ½ teaspoon/2 mL of your favorite hot sauce)

1 cup (250 mL) of blanched almonds, toasted

½ cup (125 mL) or so of extra virgin olive oil

1 cup (250 mL) of freshly grated Parmigiano-Reggiano cheese

A 5-ounce (142 g) container of baby arugula

½ teaspoon (2 mL) of salt

Lots of freshly ground pepper

PAN-ROASTED CHICKEN WITH CHICKPEAS, ORZO, BURST TOMATOES AND SPICY GREEN PESTO

When you have tasty pesto on hand, you're always within striking distance of a simple meal like this one. It's easy to boil water for pasta while you sear chicken breasts, then toss the works together at the last second for a bistro-quality dish. This simple group of flavors makes an excellent meal straight out of the pan, but it's just as tasty served as a cold salad of sorts. The pesto adds just the right touch of bright flavor to bring everything together, and the orzo holds its texture for days. MAKES ENOUGH FOR 4 MAINS OR 6 SIDES, EASILY DOUBLED

TODAY FOR TOMORROW   Make the Spicy Green Pesto ahead. • Fully cook this dish now and reheat anytime during the next several days (see Storage Tip).

Generously season the chicken breasts with salt and pepper. Splash a pool of cooking oil into a large skillet over medium-high heat. Using tongs, carefully add the chicken to the sizzling pan and sear, turning occasionally, until golden brown on both sides, 10 minutes or so. Add the tomatoes and chickpeas, lower the heat, cover and cook until the chicken is tender and just cooked through, another 5 minutes or so. Transfer the chicken to a plate and let rest for about 10 minutes. Slice thinly.

Meanwhile, cook the orzo. Bring a large full pot of salted water to a vigorous boil. Add the orzo and cook until al dente, no more than 10 minutes. Drain thoroughly, retaining a few splashes of cooking water in the pot. Return the pasta to the cooking pot along with the pesto, tomato mixture and the sliced chicken. Toss thoroughly and serve.

2 boneless, skinless chicken breasts

½ teaspoon (2 mL) of salt

Lots of freshly ground pepper

2 tablespoons (30 mL) or so of vegetable oil

2 pints (1 L) of cherry or grape tomatoes

A 19-ounce (540 mL) can of chickpeas, drained and well rinsed

1 cup (250 mL) of orzo

1 cup (250 mL) of Spicy Green Pesto (page 177)

STORAGE TIP

Refrigerate: Tightly seal leftovers and refrigerate within 30 minutes of cooking. Store for up to 4 days before reheating.

PAN-BAKED SALMON WITH FENNEL AND SPICY GREEN PESTO

There are few ways to cook salmon more delicious than this one. The bold, aromatic pesto brightens the fennel's anise flavors. This cooking method is designed to capture all the fish's flavorful cooking juices. MAKES ENOUGH FOR 4 TO 6 MAINS, EASILY DOUBLED

TODAY FOR TOMORROW Make the Spicy Green Pesto ahead. • Prepare the flavor base for this fish a few days in advance, ready to finish with fresh fish (see Storage Tip).

FOR THE FLAVOR BASE

2 tablespoons (30 mL) or so of extra virgin olive oil

1 large fennel bulb, trimmed and thinly sliced

1 red onion, thinly sliced

1 tablespoon (15 mL) of fennel seeds

The zest and juice of ½ lemon

2 tablespoons (30 mL) of Pernod or other anise-flavored liqueur (optional)

½ teaspoon (2 mL) of salt

Lots of freshly ground pepper

FOR THE FISH

4 to 6 fresh skinless salmon fillets (4 ounces/115 g each) or your favorite firm-fleshed fish

½ cup (125 mL) or more of Spicy Green Pesto (page 177)

Preheat your oven to 375°F (190°C). Turn on your convection fan if you have one.

Prepare the flavor base. Match your favorite large, heavy skillet or sauté pan with a tight-fitting lid and set it over medium-high heat. Splash in the oil. Add the fennel, red onion and fennel seeds and sauté until the fennel and onion soften, 5 minutes or so. Turn off the heat and stir in the lemon zest and juice, Pernod (if using), salt and pepper.

Prepare the salmon. Pat dry the fish with paper towel. Arrange the fillets on a large plate and top each one with 2 tablespoons (30 mL) of pesto. Use your fingers to thoroughly massage each piece with the aromatic pesto.

Nestle the fillets into the fennel mixture. Cover tightly and bake until the fish is tender, 20 minutes or so. Serve with simple rice.

STORAGE TIP

Refrigerate: Tightly seal the flavor base and refrigerate within 30 minutes of cooking. Store for up to 5 days. Fresh fish is best cooked soon after it's purchased. Tightly seal leftovers and refrigerate for up to 4 days before reheating.

PENNE WITH GREEN VEGGIES AND SPICY GREEN PESTO

This vegetarian dish is so packed with protein and flavor that no one at the table will notice anything missing—they'll be too busy eating their vegetables. Cooked pasta continues to absorb moisture, so leftovers can be soggy, and pesto heated twice loses its freshness. Better to encourage seconds!

MAKES A LARGE POT, ENOUGH FOR 4 TO 6 MEALS, EASILY DOUBLED

TODAY FOR TOMORROW   Make the Spicy Green Pesto ahead. • Prep the broccoli ahead, tightly seal in a zip-top bag and refrigerate.

Bring a large pot of salted water to a furious boil. Toss in the pasta, lower the heat to a steady simmer and cook for 5 minutes. Stir in the broccoli and green beans, return to a simmer and cook until the pasta is al dente, another 5 minutes or so. Stir in the peas, give them a minute to heat through, then drain the works, retaining a few splashes of cooking water in the pot. Stir the pesto into the hot water. Return the pasta to the pot and stir in the spinach.

STORAGE TIP

Refrigerate: Tightly seal leftovers and refrigerate within 30 minutes of cooking. Store for up to 4 days before reheating.

1 pound (450 g) of penne or your favorite pasta

1 large head of broccoli, trimmed into florets

A handful or two of fresh or frozen green beans, cut into bite-size lengths

1 cup (250 mL) of frozen peas or frozen shelled edamame

1 cup (250 mL) or more of Spicy Green Pesto (page 177)

A 5-ounce (142 g) container of baby spinach

RIPE TOMATO SALSA

There are as many recipes for classic tomato salsa as there are cooks to make it. The best are packed with sharply seasoned, deep yet fresh tomato flavor. Here's my simple take and twist on the kitchen classic: a double tomato approach, bold spice flavors and smoky heat. This salsa pulls its weight: tasty and easy to cook with, nice and thick, with reliably strong flavor. Salsa is at its best after the flavors have had a few days to blend. MAKES 5 CUPS (1.25 L) OR SO, ENOUGH FOR A LOT OF SNACKING OR A MEAL OR TWO, EASILY DOUBLED

TODAY FOR TOMORROW Make this salsa ahead (see Storage Tip). • Use your prepared salsa for the recipes that follow: Chili-Baked Hand Chips and Fresh Salsa Dip (page 187), Salsa Cheddar Tortilla Crusted Chicken (page 188), Bacon Salsa Quesadillas (page 190).

Place a large saucepan or soup pot over medium heat. Splash in the oil and toss in the cumin, coriander and fennel seeds. Toast gently, releasing the spices' full flavors, 1 or 2 minutes. Strain the tomato juice into the pot. Gently squeeze the juice from each of the whole tomatoes, then toss the tomatoes directly into your food processor. Add the onion, garlic and chipotle chili to the pot. Briefly bring the works to a furious boil, then reduce the heat to a slow, steady simmer. Continue cooking, gently reducing and thickening the sauce, 15 minutes or so.

Stuff the cilantro into the food processor. Add the thickened sauce and the lime zest and juice. Pulse into a rustic, chunky salsa or purée into something smoother. Pour into a bowl and stir in the cherry tomatoes.

STORAGE TIP

Refrigerate: Tightly seal the salsa and refrigerate for up to a week.

Freeze: Portion the salsa, tightly seal and freeze for up to 30 days. Thaw in the refrigerator for 1 or 2 days.

2 tablespoons (30 mL) of vegetable oil

1 tablespoon (15 mL) of cumin seeds

1 tablespoon (15 mL) of coriander seeds

1 tablespoon (15 mL) of fennel seeds

A 28-ounce (796 mL) can of whole plum tomatoes, organic if possible

1 large onion, finely chopped

4 garlic cloves, smashed

1 chipotle chili in adobo sauce

Tender sprigs from 1 bunch of fresh cilantro

The zest and juice of 1 lime

1 pint (500 mL) of cherry tomatoes, quartered

CHILI-BAKED HAND CHIPS AND FRESH SALSA DIP

An amazing salsa deserves an amazing chip, and these chip dippers make any dip a special occasion. These are fun to bake and even more fun to snap off and snack on. Spicy too, with their chili honey glaze. It's just as easy to make a lot of these as a little, and they stay crisp for close to a week.   MAKES ENOUGH CRISPY CHIPS FOR 2 TO 4 TO SNACK, EASILY DOUBLED

TODAY FOR TOMORROW   Make the Ripe Tomato Salsa ahead. • Crisp the chips in advance (see Storage Tip).

Position a rack near the bottom of the oven and one near the middle. Preheat your oven to 350°F (180°C). Turn on your convection fan if you have one.

Arrange the tortillas on a pair of baking sheets. In a small bowl, whisk together the chili powder, honey and olive oil. Using your fingers or a pastry brush, thoroughly and evenly spread the mixture all over the tortillas, right to their edges. Bake, rotating the pans once, until lightly browned and crispy, 20 minutes or so. Rest until cool enough to handle, then break into manageable chips.

THE DIPPERS

8 medium white flour tortillas

1 tablespoon (15 mL) of chili powder

1 tablespoon (15 mL) of liquid honey

1 tablespoon (15 mL) of extra
   virgin olive oil

THE DIP

2 cups (500 mL) of Ripe Tomato
   Salsa (page 185)

STORAGE TIP

Room Temperature: Cool the chips completely, tightly seal in a zip-top bag and store for up to 6 days.

SALSA CHEDDAR TORTILLA CRUSTED CHICKEN

This dish is one of my favorites when I'm in a hurry. It's a flavorful anchor for any dinner and a fun way to show off a familiar group of ingredients. It's flat-out delicious every time—and a great use of your favorite make ahead salsa! MAKES ENOUGH FOR 4 MEALS, EASILY DOUBLED

TODAY FOR TOMORROW Make the Ripe Tomato Salsa ahead. • Fully cook this dish now and reheat anytime during the next several days (see Storage Tip).

2 very large boneless, skinless chicken breasts (8 ounces/225 g or more each)

1 teaspoon (5 mL) of salt

Lots of freshly ground pepper

1 cup (250 mL) of Ripe Tomato Salsa (page 185)

2 cups (500 mL) of grated cheddar or taco blend cheese

A few handfuls of crushed tortilla chips

Preheat your oven to 450°F (230°C). Turn on your convection fan if you have one. Line a baking sheet with foil or parchment paper.

Working with one chicken breast at a time, place the breast inside a heavy-duty zip-top freezer bag. Using a rolling pin or the bottom of a small pan, pound and press the chicken into a cutlet about 1/2 inch (1 cm) thick. Carefully remove from the bag, cut into 2 even portions and arrange on the baking sheet.

Generously season the chicken pieces with salt and pepper. Top each piece evenly with 1/4 cup (60 mL) of the salsa, then 1/2 cup (125 mL) or so of cheese. Finish with a handful of crushed tortilla chips. Bake until the chicken is tender and the chips begin to brown and crisp, 15 to 20 minutes.

STORAGE TIP

Freeze: Tightly seal the cooked chicken individually and freeze for 30 days or more. Reheat straight from the freezer or thaw in the refrigerator for 1 or 2 days before reheating. Tightly seal leftovers and refrigerate for up to 4 days before reheating.

BACON SALSA QUESADILLAS

Quesadillas are deceptively simple to make. They're so easy to throw together and pop into the oven that you always end up pleasantly surprised by their crispy, cheesy deliciousness. That's usually when you start planning your next batch. MAKES 4 QUESADILLAS, ENOUGH FOR 4 MEALS, EASILY DOUBLED

TODAY FOR TOMORROW Make the Ripe Tomato Salsa ahead. • Prepare this dish in advance, ready to bake when the time comes (see Storage Tip). • Fully cook this dish now and reheat anytime during the next several days (see Storage Tip).

8 thick slices of bacon, cut into thin strips

8 large white flour tortillas

A few splashes of vegetable oil

2 cups (500 mL) of Ripe Tomato Salsa (page 185)

1 cup (250 mL) or more of grated cheddar cheese

1 cup (250 mL) or more of grated Monterey Jack cheese

Position a rack near the bottom of the oven and one near the middle. Preheat your oven to 425°F (220°C). Turn on your convection fan if you have one. Line 2 baking sheets with parchment paper or foil.

Toss the bacon and a big splash of water into a large skillet over medium-high heat. Cook until the bacon is fully browned and evenly crispy, 10 minutes or so. Pour off none, some or all of the fat.

Lightly brush 4 tortillas with vegetable oil or bacon fat. Flip onto the baking sheet, oiled side down. Evenly top each one with 1/2 cup (125 mL) of salsa and its fair share of bacon bits and drippings. Cover with 1/4 cup (60 mL) each of the two cheeses (reserving a little for the top of the quesadillas). Place another tortilla on top of the works, press it down gently and brush thoroughly and evenly with more vegetable oil or bacon fat. Sprinkle the quesadillas with the reserved cheese.

Bake, without rotating the racks, until the quesadillas are golden brown and crisp, 10 minutes or so. Cut into wedges and serve.

STORAGE TIP

Refrigerate: Tightly seal the prepared quesadillas and refrigerate for up to 3 days before cooking. • Tightly seal leftovers and refrigerate for up to 4 days before reheating.

TEX-MEX CHIPOTLE CHICKEN FILLING

Tex-Mex joints all have a variety of meaty fillings like this one on their menus packed with big, bright Tex-Mex flavors ready to roll into any type of tortilla. Burritos, enchiladas, quesadillas, crispy tacos, soft tacos, tostadas, rotis—what will you roll? MAKES 4 CUPS (1 L) OR SO OF FILLING, ENOUGH FOR 8 TO 10 BURRITOS OR ENCHILADAS OR 18 TACOS, EASILY DOUBLED

TODAY FOR TOMORROW Make this filling ahead (see Storage Tip). • Use your prepared filling for the recipes that follow: Chipotle Chicken Burritos with Cilantro Sriracha Sour Cream (page 195), Chipotle Chicken Enchiladas (page 196), Chipotle Chicken Tacos with Pico de Gallo (page 198).

Preheat your oven to 350°F (180°C). Turn on your convection fan if you have one.

Match a Dutch oven or heavy soup pot with a tight-fitting lid and set it over medium-high heat. Generously season the chicken with salt and pepper. Splash a thin pool of vegetable oil into the pan. Using tongs, carefully add the chicken to the sizzling pan and sear, turning occasionally, until golden on all sides, 10 minutes or so. Transfer the chicken to a plate.

Add the onions, garlic, chili powder, cumin and oregano to the pan and sauté briefly. Stir in the tomatoes, corn, beans and chipotle chilies. Briefly bring to a furious boil, then reduce the heat to a slow, steady simmer. Nestle in the seared chicken.

Cover, transfer to the oven and bake until the chicken is so tender that it falls off the bones, an hour and 15 minutes or so. Gently ease the bones and cartilage out of each thigh and stir the meat back into the sauce.

8 bone-in, skinless chicken thighs

½ teaspoon (2 mL) of salt

Lots of freshly ground pepper

A few splashes of vegetable oil

1 or 2 onions, finely chopped

4 or 5 garlic cloves, minced

1 tablespoon (15 mL) of chili powder

1 tablespoon (15 mL) of ground cumin

1 tablespoon (15 mL) of dried oregano

A 28-ounce (796 mL) can of diced tomatoes

2 cups (500 mL) of frozen corn

A 14-ounce (398 mL) can of black beans, drained and well rinsed

1 or 2 chipotle chilies in adobo sauce, mashed with a fork

STORAGE TIP

Refrigerate: Tightly seal the finished filling and refrigerate within 30 minutes of cooking. Store for up to 3 days.

Freeze: Portion the finished filling, tightly seal and freeze for up to 30 days. Reheat straight from the freezer or thaw in the refrigerator for 1 or 2 days before reheating. Tightly seal leftovers and store in the refrigerator for just a few days.

CHIPOTLE CHICKEN BURRITOS WITH CILANTRO SRIRACHA SOUR CREAM

A stuffed and rolled tortilla is a burrito. Tortillas are the second most popular packaged bread in North America. They're gaining fast on number one: good old-fashioned sliced bread. Tortillas are quick, easy, inexpensive, tasty and often much healthier than plain white bread. And of course burritos are way more exciting! A FULL BATCH OF TEX-MEX CHIPOTLE CHICKEN FILLING WILL STUFF 12 TO 16 LARGE BURRITOS, EASILY DOUBLED

TODAY FOR TOMORROW   Make the Tex-Mex Chipotle Chicken Filling ahead. • Make the sour cream mixture a few days in advance. Seal and refrigerate. • Prep the veggies and cheese now so you'll be ready to roll burritos anytime in the next few days. Refrigerate tightly sealed in zip-top bags.

Stir the sour cream ingredients together and divide into 4 small dipping bowls or a festive squeeze bottle.

Reheat the Tex-Mex filling in a microwave. Lay a tortilla on your work surface. Pile the filling just below the middle of the tortilla. Top with cheese, lettuce, tomato, green onion and cilantro. Fold in the sides and roll tightly into a firm burrito. Serve with the zippy sour cream.

STORAGE TIP

Refrigerate: Burritos are best enjoyed freshly made, but leftovers can be tightly sealed and refrigerated for up to 3 days.

FOR THE SOUR CREAM (MAKES ENOUGH FOR 4 BURRITOS)

1 cup (250 mL) of sour cream

1 tablespoon (15 mL) of Sriracha sauce

A handful of finely chopped fresh cilantro

The zest and juice of ½ lime

FOR EACH BURRITO

½ cup (125 mL) or so of Tex-Mex Chipotle Chicken Filling (page 193)

1 large white flour tortilla

¼ cup (60 mL) of grated cheddar or taco blend cheese

A handful of shredded romaine lettuce

A handful of diced tomato

1 green onion, thinly sliced

A handful of tender fresh cilantro sprigs

CHIPOTLE CHICKEN ENCHILADAS

In the world of tortillas there are many ways to roll out dinner. Enchiladas are simply tortillas rolled around a savory stuffing, then baked under spicy salsa and crispy cheese. Yet another way to rock and roll your house specialty: Tex-Mex Chipotle Chicken Filling! FILLS A 13- × 9-INCH (3.5 L) PAN, ENOUGH FOR 4 TO 6 MEALS, EASILY DOUBLED

TODAY FOR TOMORROW Make the Tex-Mex Chipotle Chicken Filling ahead. • Prepare this dish in advance, ready to bake when the time comes (see Storage Tip). • Fully cook this dish now and reheat anytime during the next several days (see Storage Tip).

10 medium corn or flour tortillas

5 cups (1.25 L) or so of Tex-Mex Chipotle Chicken Filling (page 193)

3 cups (750 mL) or so of your favorite salsa

2 cups (500 mL) of grated cheddar, Monterey Jack or taco blend cheese

Preheat your oven to 375°F (190°C). Turn on your convection fan if you have one.

Lay the tortillas on your work surface. Spoon ½ cup (125 mL) or so of Tex-Mex filling down the middle of each tortilla. Roll up tightly and arrange in a 13- × 9-inch (3.5 L) baking pan, neatly filling it. Spoon the salsa evenly over the tops and sprinkle evenly with the cheese. Bake until heated through and lightly browned, 30 minutes or so. Serve with a margarita or two!

STORAGE TIP

Refrigerate: These enchiladas can be filled, rolled, tightly sealed and refrigerated for up to 3 days before cooking. • Tightly seal leftovers and refrigerate within 30 minutes of cooking. Store for up to 3 days before reheating.

Freeze: Roll and top the enchiladas, tightly seal and freeze for up to 30 days. Cook straight from the freezer or thaw in the refrigerator for a day or so before reheating. Tightly seal leftovers and store in the refrigerator for just a few days.

CHIPOTLE CHICKEN TACOS WITH PICO DE GALLO

Taco night will never be the same after you start skipping the standard spicy boring hamburger business and start stuffing some serious flavor into the works. Your Tex-Mex filling is awesome for tacos, especially when it's topped with the familiar flavors of a more-salad-than-salsa classic, pico de gallo. HALF A BATCH OF TEX-MEX CHIPOTLE CHICKEN FILLING STUFFS 12 TO 16 TACOS, ENOUGH FOR 4 TO 6 MEALS, EASILY DOUBLED

TODAY FOR TOMORROW Make the Tex-Mex Chipotle Chicken Filling ahead. • Make the pico de gallo ahead (see Storage Tip).

FOR THE PICO DE GALLO

2 ripe Roma tomatoes, finely diced

2 green onions, thinly sliced

2 garlic cloves, finely minced

A handful of finely chopped
   fresh cilantro

The zest and juice of 1 lime

½ teaspoon (2 mL) of your
   favorite hot sauce

¼ teaspoon (1 mL) of salt

FOR THE TACOS

1 head of iceberg or Bibb lettuce

12 small soft white flour tortillas

12 small crisp yellow corn taco
   shells, lightly toasted

3 to 4 cups (750 mL to 1 L) of
   Tex-Mex Chipotle Chicken Filling
   (page 193), reheated

8 ounces (225 g) or so of grated
   cheddar or taco blend cheese

Make the pico de gallo. Toss all the ingredients together. Done!

Make the tacos. Lay a large lettuce leaf over a small flour tortilla. Wrap both around a crisp taco. Stuff each one with ¼ cup (60 mL) of Tex-Mex filling. Top with a generous sprinkle of cheese and a couple of spoonfuls of pico de gallo. Fold firmly, knowing that when the inner crisp taco inevitably cracks, it'll be held together by the flexible outer layers.

STORAGE TIP

Refrigerate: Tightly seal the pico de gallo and refrigerate for up to 4 days before Taco Night.

HOMEMADE CHICKEN BROTH

Homemade chicken broth is the ultimate make ahead stash. True homemade broth is dramatically superior to store-bought stock. Just a few cups can anchor and add richness to so many other dishes. The best way to craft a batch from a whole chicken is in a pressure cooker, gear worth having even if the only thing you ever use it for is homemade chicken broth. Of course if you don't have one, just use a pot. Broiling the chicken doubles the broth's flavor and body. MAKES 8 CUPS (2 L) OR SO, ENOUGH TO BUILD SEVERAL DISHES OR MAKE 4 TO 6 BOWLS OF SOUP OR STEW, EASILY DOUBLED

TODAY FOR TOMORROW Make this broth ahead (see Storage Tip). • Use your prepared broth for the recipes that follow: Old-Fashioned Chicken Noodle Soup (page 203), Slow Cooker French Onion Soup with Rye and Gruyère (page 204), Louisiana Chicken Stew (page 207).

Cut the chicken into 10 pieces (or have your butcher do it for you): 2 wings, 2 thighs, 2 drumsticks, and 2 breasts each cut in half.

Brown the chicken. Position a rack near the top of the oven and preheat your broiler. Turn on your convection fan if you have one. Arrange a single layer of the chicken pieces in a large skillet, douse them with a few splashes of oil, turning and rubbing until they're evenly coated. Broil, turning occasionally, until evenly and thoroughly browned, 15 minutes or so. Keep an eye on things and avoid any blackening—it makes the broth bitter. If things start to get out of control, add a splash of water to slow the works down.

Transfer the browned chicken with its cooking juices and drippings into your pressure cooker or a large soup pot. Fill the skillet with some of the water, gently swirling to dissolve the browned flavor. Rest for a few minutes to fully dissolve the works, then scrape every last bit of goodness into the pressure cooker or pot.

Add the remaining water, the onions, carrots, celery, garlic, bay leaves, thyme, salt and peppercorns. Briefly bring to a furious boil, then reduce the heat to a slow, steady simmer. Lock the pressure cooker lid and cook until the chicken's richness and aromatic flavors fully dissolve into the broth, 45 minutes. Alternatively, cover the pot tightly and simmer for 2 hours or so.

Remove from the heat and rest the proceeds for about half an hour. Strain through a fine-mesh strainer into a large container. Pick through the solids and reserve as much shredded meat as you can; discard the remaining solids. Transfer the broth to smaller storage containers as needed. Refrigerate until the fat congeals. The fat may be discarded if you like or kept for maximum flavor.

1 large chicken or 24 full chicken wings

A few splashes of vegetable oil

12 cups (3 L) of water

2 or 3 large onions, thinly sliced

2 or 3 large carrots, thinly sliced

2 or 3 celery stalks, thinly sliced

Cloves from 1 head of garlic, smashed

2 or 3 bay leaves

4 or 5 sprigs of fresh thyme

1 tablespoon (15 mL) of salt

½ teaspoon (2 mL) of black peppercorns

STORAGE TIP

Refrigerate: Tightly seal the broth and the reserved meat separately and refrigerate within 30 minutes of cooking. Store for up to 6 days before using.

Freeze: Portion the broth and reserved meat separately, tightly seal and freeze for a month or more. Reheat straight from the freezer or thaw in the refrigerator for a day or so before reheating. Tightly seal leftovers and store in the refrigerator for just a few days before reheating.

OLD-FASHIONED CHICKEN NOODLE SOUP

Homemade chicken noodle soup is the ultimate comfort food. This is an essential dish for its healing power and morale restoration. Perhaps it's worth freezing a few bowls of this goodness as back-up medicine. You can quickly thaw to help chase away any chilly winter sniffles. Its secret is the true richness of the underlying homemade broth. The slurpy noodles don't hurt either! MAKES ENOUGH FOR 4 TO 6 BOWLS, EASILY DOUBLED

TODAY FOR TOMORROW Make Homemade Chicken Broth ahead. • Prep the vegetables a few days in advance. Refrigerate tightly sealed in a zip-top bag. • Fully cook this soup now and reheat anytime during the next several days (see Storage Tip).

Splash the oil into a large soup pot over medium-high heat. Add the onions, carrots, celery and garlic. Sauté until they soften, 5 minutes or so. Season along the way with salt and pepper.

Add the chicken broth, thyme, your choice of noodles and the reserved chicken. Briefly bring the works to a furious boil, then reduce the heat to a slow, steady simmer. Cook until the udon noodles are heated through, a minute or two, or until the pasta is al dente, 10 minutes or so.

STORAGE TIP

Refrigerate: Tightly seal and refrigerate within 30 minutes of cooking. Store for up to 6 days before reheating.

Freeze: Portion, tightly seal and store for up to 30 days. Reheat straight from the freezer or thaw in the refrigerator for 1 or 2 days before reheating. Tightly seal leftovers and store in the refrigerator for just a few days.

2 tablespoons (30 mL) of vegetable oil

1 or 2 large onions, finely chopped

1 or 2 large carrots, finely diced or shredded

1 or 2 celery stalks, thinly sliced

2 or 3 garlic cloves, smashed

1½ teaspoons (7 mL) of salt

Lots of freshly ground pepper

1 full batch of Homemade Chicken Broth (page 201)

Leaves from 4 or 5 sprigs of fresh thyme

A 7-ounce (200 g) package of cooked udon noodles or an equivalent amount of dried spaghetti or other long, slurpy noodles, even macaroni

2 cups (500 mL) or so of reserved cooked chicken

SLOW COOKER FRENCH ONION SOUP WITH RYE AND GRUYÈRE

You can taste patience in a bowl of French onion soup. The flavors simply can't be rushed. It takes time to slowly melt the onions into rich, caramelized goodness, the foundation of any good French onion soup. Incomparable flavor crafted with your Homemade Chicken Broth. A truly delicious soup. MAKES ENOUGH FOR 6 TO 8 BOWLS, NOT EASILY DOUBLED BUT YOU CAN DO IT IN BATCHES

TODAY FOR TOMORROW   Make Homemade Chicken Broth ahead. • Slice the onions up to 3 days in advance. Refrigerate tightly sealed in a zip-top bag. • Fully cook this soup now and reheat anytime during the next several days (see Storage Tip).

8 to 10 large yellow onions
  (3 to 4 pounds/1.3 to 1.8 kg),
  thinly sliced

1 teaspoon (5 mL) of salt

Lots of freshly ground pepper

¼ cup (60 mL) of butter, melted

1 full batch of Homemade Chicken
  Broth (page 201)

½ cup (125 mL) of sherry, brandy,
  Madeira or marsala

Leaves from 4 or 5 sprigs of fresh
  thyme

6 to 8 thick slices of rustic rye bread,
  trimmed to fit the bowls and
  toasted

1 pound (450 g) or so of Gruyère
  cheese, grated (6 to 8 cups/
  1.5 to 2 L)

Stuff your slow cooker with the sliced onions, sprinkle in the salt and pepper and drizzle in the melted butter. Cover tightly and cook on low for 10 hours or so, stirring once or twice. The onions will wilt, concentrate, caramelize and thicken.

Transfer the onions to a soup pot. Add the chicken broth, sherry and thyme. Briefly bring the works to a furious boil, then reduce the heat to a slow, steady simmer while you ready your heatproof soup bowls.

Preheat your broiler. Turn on your convection fan if you have one. Fill each bowl to within an inch (2.5 cm) or so of the rim. Fit in and float the rye bread. Carefully cover with a mound of the cheese. Broil until the cheese is thoroughly melted and golden brown, no more than 5 minutes. Keep an eye on the works so the cheese doesn't blacken and become bitter.

STORAGE TIP

Refrigerate: Tightly seal leftovers and refrigerate within 30 minutes of cooking. Store for up to 4 days before reheating.

Freeze: Portion, tightly seal and store for up to 30 days. Reheat straight from the freezer or thaw in the refrigerator for a day or so before reheating. Tightly seal leftovers and refrigerate for up to 4 days before reheating.

LOUISIANA CHICKEN STEW

The flavors of the famous Creole cooking of New Orleans and the spicy Cajun cooking of the surrounding countryside bring big, bold, bright flavor to this classic stew. You can make a dish like this with water and it will satisfy, but it's ten times better with your own Homemade Chicken Broth. There's no substitute for old-school rich, real savory flavors.   MAKES A BIG POTFUL, ENOUGH FOR 12 LARGE BOWLS, 2 OR 3 MEALS, EASILY DOUBLED

TODAY FOR TOMORROW   Make the Homemade Chicken Broth ahead. • Prep the vegetables a few days in advance. Refrigerate tightly sealed in a zip-top bag. • Fully cook this dish now and reheat anytime during the next several days (see Storage Tip).

Pour the oil into a large soup pot over medium-high heat. While whisking, slowly sprinkle in the flour. Continue whisking until the paste browns to the color of peanut butter, about 10 minutes.

Stir in the garlic, paprika, oregano, thyme, salt and cayenne. Toss in the Holy Trinity of Creole cooking—the onions, green peppers and celery. Cook, stirring, until the vegetables soften, 5 minutes or so. Slowly stir in the chicken broth, continuing to stir as it heats and thickens. Stir in the tomatoes, okra, chorizo and chicken meat. Briefly bring the works to a furious boil, then reduce the heat to a slow, steady simmer. Cook for another 10 minutes or so.

STORAGE TIP

Refrigerate: Tightly seal and refrigerate within 30 minutes of cooking. Store for up to 4 days before reheating.

Freeze: Portion, tightly seal and store for up to 30 days. Reheat straight from the freezer or thaw in the refrigerator for 1 or 2 days before reheating. Tightly seal leftovers and refrigerate for up to 4 days before reheating.

1 cup (250 mL) of vegetable oil

1 cup (250 mL) of all-purpose flour

4 to 6 garlic cloves, minced

1 tablespoon (15 mL) of paprika

1 tablespoon (15 mL) of dried oregano

1 tablespoon (15 mL) of dried thyme

2 teaspoons (10 mL) of salt

A big pinch of cayenne

2 large onions, chopped

2 green bell peppers, halved and chopped

2 celery stalks, sliced

1 full batch of Homemade Chicken Broth (page 201)

A 28-ounce (796 mL) can of diced tomatoes

A 10-ounce (300 g) bag of sliced frozen okra

10 ounces (300 g) or so of chorizo, andouille or your favorite spicy sausage, thinly sliced

A few cups of reserved cooked chicken

A JAR OF SPICY SPICE RUB

The world of seasoning is full of spice blends conveniently mixed in advance, ready to add distinctive flavors to your cooking. This all-purpose rub is packed with a powerful punch of big, bright Tex-Mex flavor. It's an excellent way to bring some instant zip to your table. You can toss it with meat, fish or vegetables, then cook them fast or slow, with the searing heat of a live fire or in a low and slow oven. MAKES 2 CUPS (500 ML), ENOUGH FOR 4 MEALS' WORTH OF SPICE RUBBING

TODAY FOR TOMORROW Make this spice rub ahead (see Storage Tip). • Use your prepared rub for the recipes that follow: Spice Roast Salmon with Tartar Sauce (page 210), Spice Roast Root Vegetables (page 212), All-Day Roast Pork Shoulder (page 214).

Thoroughly whisk together all the ingredients.

Prep your meal. Sprinkle on just enough rub to add a thick coat of flavor. Because you're seasoning raw fish or meat, any rub that falls off will have to be discarded. You may find it easier to place the protein in a shallow baking dish to contain any errant spice and roll the works to gather up the excess.

STORAGE TIP

Room Temperature: Store in an airtight container for up to a month.

½ cup (125 mL) of brown sugar

¼ cup (60 mL) of chili powder

¼ cup (60 mL) of paprika

1 tablespoon (15 mL) of ground cumin

1 tablespoon (15 mL) of onion powder

1 tablespoon (15 mL) of garlic powder

1 tablespoon (15 mL) of ground oregano

1 tablespoon (15 mL) of salt

½ teaspoon (2 mL) of cayenne pepper

SPICE ROAST SALMON WITH TARTAR SAUCE

Love healthy salmon but a little bored with your repertoire? Try a thorough spice rubbing. Rich, fatty salmon can take it. And a spoonful of tartar sauce too. You'll be amazed at how fresh and bright your own classic tartar sauce tastes. 1 FULL BATCH OF SPICY SPICE RUB IS ENOUGH TO FLAVOR 12 SALMON FILLETS OR SO; THE TARTAR SAUCE IS EASILY DOUBLED

TODAY FOR TOMORROW Make the Spicy Spice Rub ahead. • Make the tartar sauce ahead (see Storage Tip).

FOR THE TARTAR SAUCE

1 cup (250 mL) of mayonnaise

2 tablespoons (30 mL) of capers, drained well

The zest and juice of 1 lemon

2 tablespoons (30 mL) of sweet green relish

2 green onions, thinly sliced

2 tablespoons (30 mL) of chopped fresh dill, tarragon or parsley

¼ teaspoon (1 mL) of salt

Lots of freshly ground pepper

FOR THE ROAST SALMON

4 boneless, skinless salmon fillets

A splash of vegetable oil

¼ cup (60 mL) or so of Spicy Spice Rub (page 209)

Preheat your oven to 450°F (230°C). Turn on your convection fan if you have one. Line a baking sheet or baking pan with parchment paper or foil.

Whisk together the tartar sauce ingredients. Taste and marvel at how simple it can be to craft something so classically delicious.

Place the fish fillets on a dinner plate. Splash with enough oil to lightly and evenly coat each piece, turning and rubbing with your fingers. One at a time, place the fillets on a second plate. Generously sprinkle the spice rub all over the fish. Use as much spice as you can get to stick to the fillets. Place the seasoned fillets on the baking sheet. Bake until tender and just cooked through, 15 minutes or so. Serve with the tartar sauce.

STORAGE TIP

Refrigerate: Tightly seal the tartar sauce and refrigerate for up to 4 days. • Tightly seal leftover fish and refrigerate within 30 minutes of cooking. Store for up to 3 days before reheating.

SPICE ROAST ROOT VEGETABLES

You'll have no trouble eating all your vegetables when they're this delicious! Nothing beats caramelizing the natural golden flavors of earthy sweet root veggies—and they're even better with your Spicy Spice Rub. Root vegetables take a while to cook, maybe more time than you have on a weekday night, so they're perfect candidates for making ahead, ready to reheat when needed. This dish takes well to all root vegetables: turnips, rutabaga, potatoes, sweet potatoes, parsnips, beets, onions, garlic cloves, even non-root cauliflower or fennel. MAKES ENOUGH FOR 6 TO 8 SIDES WITH LEFTOVERS, EASILY DOUBLED

TODAY FOR TOMORROW   Make the Spicy Spice Rub ahead. • Prep the vegetables a few days in advance, ready to roast when the time comes. Refrigerate tightly sealed in a zip-top bag. • Fully cook this dish now and reheat anytime during the next several days (see Storage Tip).

6 to 8 pounds (2.7 to 3.5 kg) of one or a variety of your favorite root vegetables

FOR EACH POUND (450 G) OF VEGETABLES

1 tablespoon (15 mL) or so of vegetable oil

1 tablespoon (15 mL) or so of Spicy Spice Rub (page 209)

Preheat your oven to 425°F (220°C). Turn on your convection fan if you have one.

Prep your vegetables as you wish: slice, dice or chop into large bite-size chunks. Pile the veggies into a large bowl, splash in the oil and sprinkle in the spice rub. Toss the works until every piece is lightly coated with oil and flavor. Fill a baking pan or two and roast, stirring occasionally, until tender and evenly caramelized, 30 to 45 minutes. Cooking time will vary depending on type and size, so keep an eye on things.

STORAGE TIP

Refrigerate: Tightly seal leftovers and refrigerate within 30 minutes of cooking. Store for up to 4 days before reheating.

ALL-DAY ROAST PORK SHOULDER

There are two secrets to the intensely delicious flavor of this meltingly tender, slowly roasted pork shoulder: your Spicy Spice Rub and time. Nothing beats rubbing strong vibrant flavors onto tough meat, then sitting back as the works slowly cook until the meat falls right off the bone. MAKES ENOUGH FOR 4 TO 6 MAINS OR 8 TO 10 SANDWICHES, EASILY DOUBLED

TODAY FOR TOMORROW Make the Spicy Spice Rub ahead. • Fully cook this dish now and reheat or enjoy sliced cold in sandwiches anytime during the next several days (see Storage Tip).

3 or 4 large onions, thinly sliced

1 large skinless, bone-in pork shoulder or blade roast (5 pounds/2.25 kg or so), tied or not

A splash or two of vegetable oil

¼ cup (60 mL) or more of Spicy Spice Rub (page 209)

Preheat your oven to 400°F (200°C). Turn on your convection fan if you have one.

Place a pile of onions in the middle of a roasting pan or baking pan. Rinse the pork shoulder and pat it dry. Using your sharpest knife, carefully score the fat on the top of the pork in a deep diamond pattern, cutting all the way through the fat but not into the meat beneath. Rub the shoulder all over with vegetable oil, lightly and evenly coating it. Sprinkle on the spice rub, turning and rubbing until the roast is thoroughly coated with flavor. Nestle fat side up into the onions, spreading them out a bit.

Bake, uncovered, for 30 minutes. Meanwhile, place one long sheet of foil over another one the same length. Fold over one long side by ½ inch (1 cm) or so and crimp tightly, then fold and crimp another ½ inch. Open up the two sheets into one larger one and tightly crease the center seam.

Lower the temperature to 250°F (120°C). Cover the pork very tightly with the foil and continue baking until meltingly tender, 6 to 8 hours. You can do one of two things at this point. With two pairs of tongs, ease out the blade bone and shred the meat, mixing it into the onions and pan drippings, to stuff into sandwiches. Or you can present as a roast, slicing at the table and serving the onions and drippings on the side.

STORAGE TIP

Refrigerate: Tightly seal leftovers and refrigerate within 30 minutes of cooking. Store for up to 4 days.

Freeze: Portion the cooked roast, tightly seal and freeze for up to 30 days. Reheat straight from the freezer or thaw in the refrigerator for 1 or 2 days before reheating.

DESSERTS AND TREATS

DESSERTS AND TREATS RECIPES

HOMEMADE SODA POP

Fresh, local pop is back! It's trendy to charge your own soda water, maybe because at home you can stir in way more flavor and a lot less sugar. It's easy to craft a creative flavor base or two ahead of time so you're ready to enjoy a cool, delicious, guilt-free treat any time you like. You'll need a soda machine and there are lots of reasonably priced machines available. Otherwise, you can use bottled sparkling water.   EACH SYRUP MAKES ENOUGH FOR 6 TO 8 POPS, EASILY DOUBLED

TODAY FOR TOMORROW   These syrups can be made in advance (see Storage Tip). • The Vanilla Chai and Lavender Lemon syrups need at least 12 hours of rest to fully release their flavors, and they're even better after a few days. • Soda water can be charged and chilled in advance. It holds its charge for a day or so.

RASPBERRY GINGER SYRUP

1 cup (250 mL) of sugar

½ cup (125 mL) of water

4 inches (10 cm) or so of fresh ginger, very thinly sliced

A 21-ounce (600 g) bag of frozen raspberries (or fresh ones)

FOR A COCKTAIL

1 shot (1 ounce/30 mL) of gin, vodka, anise or your favorite spirit

A few frozen raspberries

Pour the sugar and water into a small saucepan over medium-high heat. Briefly bring to a furious boil, then reduce the heat to a slow, steady simmer. Toss in the ginger slices, cover and simmer for another 5 minutes. Stir in the raspberries and continue simmering until they soften, 5 minutes. Strain through a fine-mesh strainer, pressing out every last precious drop of flavor with a rubber spatula or the back of a small ladle. Refrigerate.

Charge and chill your soda water. Pour 8 to 12 ounces (250 to 375 mL) of soda over ice and stir in 2 to 3 ounces (60 to 90 mL) of syrup.

To make a refreshing cocktail, pour 1 shot of gin, vodka, anise or your favorite spirit and a shot of raspberry syrup over ice. Top with 4 to 6 ounces (125 to 175 mL) of soda water and a few frozen raspberries.

VANILLA CHAI SYRUP

3 cups (750 mL) of water

1 cup (250 mL) of honey

20 tea bags of your favorite chai blend

2 tablespoons (30 mL) of pure vanilla extract

FOR A COCKTAIL

1 shot (1 ounce/30 mL) of Irish Cream, Fireball, anise or your favorite spirit

A pinch of ground cinnamon or freshly grated nutmeg

Pour the water and honey into a small saucepan over medium-high heat. Briefly bring to a furious boil, then reduce the heat to a slow, steady simmer. Cram the tea bags into a large heatproof jar. Pour the honey syrup over the tea bags. Splash in the vanilla. Seal tightly, refrigerate and let steep overnight.

Strain through a fine-mesh strainer, pressing out every last precious drop of flavor with a rubber spatula or the back of a small ladle.

Charge and chill your soda water. Pour 8 to 12 ounces (250 to 375 mL) of soda over ice and stir in 1 to 2 ounces (30 to 60 mL) of syrup.

To make a mysterious cocktail, pour 1 shot of Irish Cream, Fireball, anise or your favorite spirit and a shot of chai syrup over ice. Top with 4 to 6 ounces (125 to 175 mL) of soda water and a pinch of ground cinnamon or freshly grated nutmeg.

LAVENDER LEMON SYRUP

Pour the sugar and water into a small saucepan over medium-high heat. Briefly bring to a furious boil, then reduce the heat to a slow, steady simmer. Measure the lavender flowers into a large heatproof jar. Pour the syrup over the lavender and stir in the lemon zest and juice. Seal tightly, refrigerate and let steep overnight.

Strain through a fine-mesh strainer, pressing out every last precious drop of flavor with a rubber spatula or the back of a small ladle.

Charge and chill your soda water. Pour 8 to 12 ounces (250 to 375 mL) of soda over ice and stir in 1 to 2 ounces (30 to 60 mL) of syrup and the fresh lemon juice.

To make an aromatic cocktail, pour 1 shot of gin or vodka, a shot of lavender syrup and the bitters (if using) over ice. Top with 4 to 6 ounces (125 to 175 mL) of soda water and a squeeze of fresh lemon juice.

2 cups (500 mL) of sugar

2 cups (500 mL) of water

1 cup (250 mL) of dried lavender flowers

The zest and juice of 2 lemons

FOR A COCKTAIL

1 shot (1 ounce/30 mL) of gin or vodka

A dash or two of your favorite bitters (optional)

A squeeze of fresh lemon juice

STORAGE TIP

Refrigerate: Tightly seal the syrups and refrigerate for up to 30 days before mixing.

TROPICAL POPSICLES

These popsicles are a great straight-off-the-school-bus treat. They're packed with 100 percent natural tropical flavors and loaded with silky, smooth texture. Best of all, you can pop a batch in the freezer faster than you can make a summer ice cream run! MAKES ENOUGH FOR 12 POPSICLES, EASILY DOUBLED

TODAY FOR TOMORROW These popsicles can be made in advance (see Storage Tip).

2 ripe bananas

A 21-ounce (600 g) bag of frozen mango chunks

A 14-ounce (400 mL) can of coconut milk with cream

1 cup (250 mL) of plain full-fat yogurt

1 cup (250 mL) of pineapple juice

Pile all the ingredients into your blender and purée until very smooth. Pour into popsicle molds and freeze until firm. If necessary, briefly run under hot water to loosen before serving.

STORAGE TIP

Freeze: Tightly seal and freeze for up to 30 days.

FROZEN CHOCOLATE MOUSSE

When it comes to true dark chocolate, a little bit goes a long way. The higher the percentage of cacao, the deeper the flavor. That's how you pack a lot of flavor into a little bit of treat. Of course a little liqueur doesn't hurt either. Use Irish Cream, Grand Marnier, Amaretto, Kahlua, chocolate liqueur, even whiskey.

MAKES ENOUGH FOR TWELVE TO FOURTEEN ½-CUP (125 ML) MASON JARS, EASILY DOUBLED

TODAY FOR TOMORROW This mousse can be made in advance (see Storage Tip).

1 pound (450 g) of 72% (or higher) dark chocolate, broken into chunks

3 cups (750 mL) of whipping cream

¼ cup (60 mL) of chocolate-friendly liqueur

1 cup (250 mL) of sugar

1 tablespoon (15 mL) of pure vanilla extract

Nestle a small bowl over (not in) a small pot of gently simmering water. Toss in the chocolate along with 1 cup (250 mL) of the cream. Stir with a whisk until the chocolate smoothly melts into the cream. Remove from the pot, whisk in your choice of liqueur and cool to room temperature.

Meanwhile, whip the remaining 2 cups (500 mL) of cream with the sugar and vanilla until it's pillowy firm. Gently and evenly fold the whipped cream into the chocolate. Portion into jars or glass dessert dishes, tightly seal and freeze.

For a firm, frozen texture, serve straight from the freezer. For a softer, smoother feel, soften at room temperature for 30 minutes or so.

STORAGE TIP

Refrigerate: Tightly seal the mousse and refrigerate for up to 5 days before serving.

Freeze: Tightly seal and freeze for up to 30 days.

DOUBLE GINGER CHOCOLATE CHIP COOKIES

You'll love the spicy hints and bursts of flavor that both fresh and candied ginger bring to a freshly baked batch of classic chocolate chip cookies. An oven full of homemade cookies is one of the all-time great ways to fire up your make ahead machine! MAKES 3 TO 4 DOZEN COOKIES, EASILY DOUBLED

TODAY FOR TOMORROW Make the dough ahead (see Storage Tip).

Position a rack near the bottom of the oven and another near the middle. Preheat your oven to 375°F (190°C). Lightly oil 2 or 3 cookie sheets.

Toss the sugar and butter into the bowl of a stand mixer fitted with the paddle, and beat until smooth and creamy, scraping the sides of the bowl once or twice. Add the eggs, vanilla and grated ginger and beat until smoothly incorporated. Whisk together the flour, baking powder and salt. Slowly add the flour mixture to the egg mixture, beating until thoroughly combined. Stir in the chocolate chips and ginger bits.

Roll scoops of dough between your palms into 1-inch (2.5 cm) balls. Arrange neatly on the cookie sheets, leaving 3 to 4 inches (8 to 10 cm) between each cookie to allow for expansion. Press gently to flatten slightly. Bake until soft and golden brown, 12 minutes or so. Cool on racks.

STORAGE TIP

Refrigerate: Tightly seal the cookie dough and refrigerate for up to 3 days before baking.

Room Temperature: Cool the baked cookies completely, tightly seal and store at room temperature for up to 6 days.

Freeze: Tightly seal the portioned dough or baked cookies and store for up to 30 days.

1½ cups (375 mL) of brown sugar

1 cup (250 mL) of butter, softened

2 eggs

1 tablespoon (15 mL) of pure vanilla extract

2 to 3 inches (5 to 8 cm) of frozen ginger, grated

2¼ cups (550 mL) of all-purpose flour

1½ teaspoons (7 mL) of baking powder

1 teaspoon (5 mL) of salt

1 cup (250 mL) of chocolate chips

1 cup (250 mL) of finely diced candied ginger

DULCE DE LECHE COCONUT SQUARES

These squares are quite simply one of the most delicious treats I've baked in years. I love transforming a simple can of sweetened condensed milk into Latin America's wildly popular dulce de leche, literally "milk candy." Your efforts will be rewarded with a giant pan of flat-out delicious treats! MAKES A BIG PAN, ENOUGH FOR 16 TO 24 SQUARES, EASILY DOUBLED IN 2 LARGE PANS

TODAY FOR TOMORROW Make the dulce de leche up to 1 year ahead. Store at room temperature.

FOR THE DULCE DE LECHE

A 10-ounce (300 mL) can of sweetened condensed milk

1 tablespoon (15 mL) of dark rum

1 tablespoon (15 mL) of pure vanilla extract

FOR THE SQUARES

3 cups (750 mL) of unsweetened shredded coconut

2 cups (500 mL) of instant rolled oats

2 cups (500 mL) of all-purpose flour

2 teaspoons (10 mL) of baking soda

2 teaspoons (10 mL) of nutmeg

2 eggs

1½ cups (375 mL) of brown sugar

1 cup (250 mL) of butter, melted

Make the dulce de leche. Fill a large, deep pot with water and bring to a furious boil, then reduce the heat to a slow, steady simmer. Remove the label from the can of condensed milk and immerse the unopened can (or a few cans) in the pot, making sure it's fully covered with boiling water. Cover and continue cooking slowly for 3 hours. Make sure the cans are always covered by a couple of inches of water. Rest and cool to room temperature. The bland, sweet milk will have caramelized and intensified into thick, dark deliciousness.

Preheat your oven to 350°F (180°C). Lightly oil a 13- × 9-inch (3.5 L) baking pan.

For the squares, in a large bowl, whisk together the coconut, oats, flour, baking soda and nutmeg. In a second bowl, whisk the eggs, then whisk in the brown sugar and melted butter until smoothly combined. Vigorously stir the wet ingredients into the dry until thoroughly combined into a strong batter.

Spread half the batter in the baking pan, smoothing it into an even bottom layer for the squares. Bake until firm, puffed and lightly browned, 10 to 15 minutes.

Meanwhile, empty the can of dulce de leche into a bowl and whisk in the rum and vanilla. Pour evenly over the baked base. Top with the remaining batter, breaking it into small clumps with your fingers. It will spread evenly as it bakes. Bake until the topping is firm and golden brown, 15 to 20 minutes. Cool to room temperature before cutting into squares.

STORAGE TIP

Refrigerate: Tightly seal the batter and refrigerate for up to 3 days before baking.

Room Temperature: Cool the baked squares completely, tightly seal and store for up to 6 days.

Freeze: Portion the baked squares, tightly seal and freeze for up to 30 days.

CHOCOLATE BARK 101

You can easily make your own homemade chocolate treats. It's deliciously easy to stir a variety of crispy, crunchy bits into a warm pool of melted chocolate, cool and harden the works, then start snapping off homemade candy! MAKES 8 SNACKS, EASILY DOUBLED OR TRIPLED

TODAY FOR TOMORROW Make your granola and the bark ahead (see Storage Tip). • Most nuts benefit from a brief toasting in a 350°F (180°C) oven to eliminate staleness. A few days ahead, toast them for 10 minutes to freshen their flavor.

FOR DARK CHOCOLATE, ALMOND AND CHERRY BARK

- 1 pound (450 g) of dark chocolate, broken into chunks
- 8 ounces (225 g) of unsalted roasted almonds
- 8 ounces (225 g) of dried cherries
- 1 tablespoon (15 mL) of dark chocolate or colored sprinkles for garnish

FOR MILK CHOCOLATE GRANOLA BARK

- 1 pound (450 g) of milk chocolate, broken into chunks
- 1 pound (450 g) of your favorite granola
- 1 tablespoon (15 mL) of dark chocolate sprinkles or shredded coconut for garnish

FOR WHITE CHOCOLATE, CRANBERRY AND PISTACHIO BARK

- 1 pound (450 g) of white chocolate, broken into chunks
- 8 ounces (225 g) of roasted shelled pistachios
- 8 ounces (225 g) of dried cranberries
- A few spoonfuls of crumbled candy canes for garnish

Line a large baking sheet with parchment paper or foil. Nestle a medium bowl over (not in) a small pot of slowly simmering water. Toss in the chocolate. Stir with a wooden spoon until the chocolate is smoothly melted. Remove from the pot and thoroughly stir in your choice of fillings. Pour the works onto the pan, gently tilting the pan so the chocolate forms a thick puddle. Sprinkle evenly with the garnish. Cool until hardened, then break into smaller pieces.

STORAGE TIP

Room Temperature: Cool the bark completely, tightly seal and store for up to 4 days.

Refrigerate: Cool the bark completely, tightly seal and refrigerate for up to a month.

Freeze: Tightly seal and freeze for up to 6 months.

SLOW COOKER APPLE GINGER SAUCE

Cooking fresh seasonal apples with bright aromatic seasonings and a touch of sweetness-boosting sugar is a time-honored way to preserve the fruit at the peak of its flavor. Cinnamon is traditionally delicious (use a tablespoon/15 mL in this recipe), but for a sharp, snappy flavor boost, try ginger instead. MAKES 6 CUPS (1.5 L), ENOUGH FOR 12 TO 16 SNACKS, EASILY DOUBLED WITH A SECOND BORROWED SLOW COOKER

TODAY FOR TOMORROW   Make the applesauce ahead (see Storage Tip). • Get out your canning gear and safely preserve for a year or more.

Squarely cut the apples off their cores and toss into your slow cooker. Sweeten with the sugar, season with the ginger and moisten with the water. Stir a bit to coat the apples evenly. Cover and cook at any setting for at least 6 hours or so. Process through an old-fashioned food mill or a newfangled food processor.

5 pounds (2.25 kg) of mixed ripe local apples

½ cup (125 mL) of brown sugar

4 inches (10 cm) of fresh ginger, unpeeled and thinly sliced

½ cup (125 mL) of water or apple juice

STORAGE TIP

Refrigerate: Tightly seal and refrigerate within 30 minutes of cooking. Store for up to 6 days.

Freeze: Portion the applesauce, tightly seal and freeze for up to 6 months.

OUR WEDDING JARS

This tasty treat was a late-night hit at our wedding, and Chazz and I are thrilled to share it with your family. It took the ultimate in make ahead planning, though. We started it three months ahead of the big day. In the spring we froze Prince Edward Island rhubarb, then, with two months to go, froze the strawberries. A week out I pulled the frozen fruit to the fridge, and with four days to go, started cooking. On the big day I slid into the finish line with seconds to spare—and finished dessert on time too! You'll be glad to know this version is much, much easier. MAKES TWELVE 1-CUP (250 ML) WIDE-MOUTH MASON JAR TREATS, EASILY DOUBLED

TODAY FOR TOMORROW   Make the compote at least a day or two in advance so it has time to thicken. • Give the panna cotta at least an overnight rest so it can fully set and thicken.

FOR THE STRAWBERRY RHUBARB COMPOTE

A 21-ounce (600 g) bag of frozen strawberries or ripe, in-season berries

1 pound (450 g) of fresh rhubarb, cubed

1 cup (250 mL) of sugar

The zest and juice of 1 lemon

½ cup (125 mL) of red, white or sweet wine

¼ cup (60 mL) of cornstarch

FOR THE PANNA COTTA

6 cups (1.5 L) of whole milk

3 envelopes (1 tablespoon/15 mL each) of unflavored gelatin

1 cup (250 mL) of sugar

1 tablespoon (15 mL) of pure vanilla extract

½ cup (125 mL) of orange liqueur or your favorite liqueur

TO FINISH

24 crisp amaretti cookies, crumbled

Make the compote. In a medium saucepan, stir together the strawberries, rhubarb, sugar, the lemon zest and juice, and half of the wine. Simmer over medium-high heat just long enough for the fruit to soften and release its juices but not long enough to reduce or thicken, 3 or 4 minutes. Stir together a slurry of the cornstarch and the remaining wine, then drizzle and stir into the simmering fruit, stirring until it thickens the works. Turn off the heat. Divide the compote equally among twelve 1-cup (250 mL) wide-mouth mason jars or glass dessert dishes. Arrange on a tray, cover tightly and refrigerate until firm, preferably overnight.

Make the panna cotta. Measure 1 cup (250 mL) of the milk into a shallow bowl. Sprinkle the gelatin evenly over the milk and let sit for a few minutes. Meanwhile, in a medium saucepan over medium heat, stir together the remaining 5 cups (1.25 L) of milk, the sugar and vanilla. Briefly bring to a steady simmer, stirring to dissolve the sugar. Turn off the heat and splash in the liqueur. Using a small rubber spatula, scrape every bit of the gelatin mixture into the pot. Continue stirring, melting the gelatin, until the liquid no longer feels gritty between your fingers, a minute or two. Cool the mixture, stirring occasionally, 20 minutes or so. Carefully and evenly ladle over the fruit compote. Cover tightly and refrigerate overnight until firm.

Before serving, top with a thick layer of crumbled cookies.

STORAGE TIP

Refrigerate: Portion out the compote, tightly seal and refrigerate for up to 3 days. Top with the panna cotta, tightly seal and refrigerate for up to 3 days more.

ORANGE VANILLA POUND CAKE

One pound each of butter, sugar, eggs and flour. Pretty straightforward, but a good old-fashioned pound cake also makes delicious toast. It's downright addictive. Top toasted thick slices with any warm fruit and ice cream for a spectacular finish fit for any feast.   MAKES 2 LOAVES, 8 TO 10 THICK SLICES EACH

TODAY FOR TOMORROW   Bake a batch of these loaves for a week or more of treats (see Storage Tip).

Position a rack just below the middle of your oven and preheat the oven to 350°F (180°C). Lightly oil two regular 9- × 5-inch (2 L) loaf pans (or use nonstick ones).

Toss the butter and sugar into the bowl of your stand mixer and whisk at high speed, scraping the sides of the bowl occasionally, until the mixture expands into a pale fluff. Add the eggs one at a time, whisking smooth after each addition, and adding the orange zest and vanilla with the last egg. Beat until smooth. Measure in half the flour and salt. Beat until smooth. Add the remaining flour and salt. Beat until smooth one last time.

Divide the batter evenly into the loaf pans, smoothing the tops. Bake until the loaves are firm and a skewer inserted in several places emerges cleanly every time, an hour or more. Cool the loaves in the pans for 20 to 30 minutes, then tip out and cool completely.

Toast thick slices until deliciously golden brown. Serve drenched with applesauce, warm fruit compote, thick jam and/or ice cream.

- 1 pound (450 g) of butter, softened
- 2 cups (500 mL) of sugar (a pound)
- 9 eggs (another pound)
- The zest of 4 to 6 organic oranges
- 1 tablespoon (15 mL) of pure vanilla extract
- 3¼ cups (810 mL) of all-purpose flour (the final pound)
- 1 teaspoon (5 mL) of salt

STORAGE TIP

Room Temperature: Cool the loaves, tightly seal and store for up to 6 days.

Refrigerate: Cool the loaves completely, tightly seal and refrigerate for up to 10 days.

Freeze: Portion, tightly seal and freeze for up to 30 days. Toast straight from the freezer or thaw in the refrigerator for 1 or 2 days.

PINEAPPLE CARROT CAKE WITH COCONUT RUM FROSTING

The best for last: Canada's favorite cake, inspired by a humble root vegetable. Thickly frosted, moist and firm, deeply spiced and absolutely delicious. Classic flavors at their best. MAKES A LARGE 16-SLICE CAKE, EASILY DOUBLED IN 2 CAKE PANS

TODAY FOR TOMORROW Bake this cake and rest it, tightly sealed, on your counter for several days of snacking.
• Make the frosting in advance (see Storage Tip).

FOR THE CAKE

- 2 cups (500 mL) of all-purpose flour
- 2 teaspoons (10 mL) of baking powder
- 1 teaspoon (5 mL) of baking soda
- 1 tablespoon (15 mL) of cinnamon
- 1 teaspoon (5 mL) of ground ginger
- ½ teaspoon (2 mL) of allspice
- ½ teaspoon (2 mL) of salt
- 3 eggs
- 1½ cups (375 mL) of brown sugar
- ¾ cup (175 mL) of vegetable oil
- 2 tablespoons (30 mL) of pure vanilla extract
- 2 large carrots, grated (about 2 cups/500 mL)
- A 14-ounce (398 mL) can of crushed pineapple, drained

FOR THE FROSTING AND FINISHING

- An 8-ounce (250 g) package of cream cheese, softened
- ½ cup (125 mL) of butter, softened
- 2 cups (500 mL) of icing sugar
- 2 tablespoons (30 mL) of dark rum
- 1 teaspoon (5 mL) of pure vanilla extract
- 1 cup (250 mL) of sweetened shredded coconut

Position a rack just below the middle of your oven and preheat the oven to 350°F (180°C). Turn on your convection fan if you have one. Lightly oil a 13- × 9-inch (3.5 L) cake pan. Lightly dust with flour, tapping out any excess.

Make the cake. In a medium bowl, whisk together the flour, baking powder, baking soda, cinnamon, ginger, allspice and salt. In the bowl of your stand mixer, combine the eggs, brown sugar, oil and vanilla. Whisk at high speed, scraping down the sides occasionally, until smoothly blended. Add about a third of the flour mixture. Beat until smooth. Measure in another third. Beat until smooth. Add the remaining flour mixture. Beat until smooth one last time. Stir in the carrots and pineapple. Pour the batter into the prepared pan.

Bake until firm, lightly browned and a skewer inserted in several places emerges cleanly every time, an hour or more. Cool the cake completely in the pan before frosting.

Make the frosting. In the bowl of your stand mixer fitted with the paddle, beat together the cream cheese and butter until smoothly blended. Add the icing sugar, rum and vanilla and beat until smooth. Finally, add the coconut and mix briefly to incorporate. Use a rubber spatula to spread the frosting thickly and evenly on the cooled cake.

STORAGE TIP

Room Temperature: Tightly seal the cake and store for up to 5 days.

Refrigerate: Tightly seal the frosting and refrigerate for up to 10 days.

Freeze: Tightly seal the frosted or unfrosted cake and freeze for up to 30 days. It thaws quickly on the counter.

THANKS

It takes a team of dedicated pros to create a cookbook. I'm thankful for everyone's contribution and proud to have my name on the cover. None of us is as good as all of us …

Thank you, Culinart Limited, to everyone who joins me every day as we help Canadians master their food lifestyle. Maureen, Edna, Vanessa, Shannon and Loretta all have a starring role in our grand production, while Tiffany guides our words and flavors. Thank you Neng-Sang Tong (Tiffany's grandmother) for so graciously sharing her pot stickers with us all.

Thank you, Andrea and your team of passionate Penguin pros, for your patient vision. I treasure our collaboration and what we've achieved together. Thank you, Ryan, Madeleine, Noah and your team, for your stunning photos. They inspire me and everyone who opens this book.

Thank you, Prince Edward Island, and to all who make it so special. We are truly blessed to call this place home, to live, work and thrive here.

Thank you to my incredibly patient family, to my wonderful wife, Chazz, and our kids, Gabe, Ariella and Camille. They are my guinea pigs and graciously endure my flavorful flights of fancy. Of course my kids are only too happy to immediately share their direct feedback. Let's just say I always know where I stand!

And thank YOU for joining us all as you cook for your friends and family!

INDEX

SOUPS, STEWS AND SLOW COOKING RECIPES

55

57

58

60

63

64

67

68

71

73

74

76

78

83

**DINNER DISHES
RECIPES**

85

88

90

93

95

96

98

103

104

106

132

134

139

VEGETABLES, GRAINS AND SIDES RECIPES

141

142

145

147

148

151

153

154

156

READY TO GO
RECIPES

158

160

163

167

169

171

172

175

177

179

180

183

209

210

212

214

219

DESSERTS
AND TREATS
RECIPES

220

222

224

227

228

231

233

234

237

239